QUIET TIME

Daily Devotional for Early Learners ages 4-6

GOPHER BUDDIES

Gopher Buddies Quiet Time

One year daily devotional for Early Learners ages 4-6

Published by Word of Life Local Church Ministries
A division of Word of Life Fellowship, Inc.
Joe Jordan - Executive Director
Jack Wyrtzen & Harry Bollback - Founders
Mike Calhoun - VP of Local Church Ministries

USA
P.O. Box 600
Schroon Lake, NY 12870
1-888-932-5827
talk@wol.org

Canada
RR#8/Owen Sound
ON, Canada N4K 5W4
1-800-461-3503 or (519) 376-3516
lcm@wol.ca

Web Address: www.wol.org

Publisher's Acknowledgements
Writers and Contributors: Jen Armstrong, Anita Eger, Gretchen Gregory, Jen Huntington, Lisa Reichard, Shirley Richards
Editor: Lisa Reichard
Curriculum Manager: Don Reichard
Design and layout: Sally Robison

ISBN - 978-1-931235-29-7
Printed in the United States of America

A note to parents

This *Quiet Time* is a great opportunity to help your child develop a relationship with God. Enjoy having fun with your child as you explore the Bible together. Each day lists a Scripture passage for you to read to your child. Next, you share the instructions for one of the many learning activities that will help your child develop key skills as they learn. Finally, you read the **I Can Pray** section to your child as you begin to teach them how to pray. What a wonderful time you will share with each other as you have a quiet time together.

Here are some tips to help your child with their quiet time:

1. Have a pencil and crayons available for activities.

2. Sit down together at a regular time each day.

3. Use the Bible to look up references with your child.

4. Talk through the activity and personal application.

5. Complete the week by documenting how many days were completed and writing an encouraging note.

Family Devotions

Word of Life publishes a *Quiet Time* for all age groups. Each *Quiet Time* uses the same Scripture passage for the week. This makes it easier for your whole family to discuss the Word of God together.

God loves you and wants to spend time with you!

Parent's Note: Read this section to your child.

A quiet time is a special time that you have each day to learn more about God and how He wants you to live. During this time, God speaks to you through His Holy Word, the Bible, and you speak to God through prayer. What an exciting adventure! Having this time every day with God will help you grow closer to Him.

Your *Quiet Time* will help you have this time each day with God. Every day you will have a Bible verse read to you. After you listen to the verse, there is a fun activity for you to do. Then you can spend a special time with God in prayer.

THE BIBLE SAYS

Psalm 7:1

SATURDAY

I CAN KNOW

Begin by reading the Scripture passage to your child.

You can ask God for help. Nothing is too hard for Him.

Next, read the "I CAN KNOW" text and discuss it with your child.

I CAN LEARN

Draw a ⭕ around what you need God's help [with]
an ✗ over the things that you already know how [to do]

Then, read the instructions for "I CAN LEARN".

On Saturdays, count the days completed for the week and write the number in the circle. Write encouraging comments (and read them to your child). Take time to award a sticker.

Lastly, read the "I CAN PRAY" statement to your child and pray together.

WAY TO GO!

WEEK #1

I CAN PRAY

Ask God to help you obey and be kind to others.

19

4

Meet Your Gopher Buddies

Introducing the Gopher family! Dad, Mom, Andy and Emily want to go with you on your adventure this year. Together, you can dig deeper in God's Word.

Spending time with God in prayer

Keeping a personal prayer diary will help you to remember to pray for people and their needs. It also reminds you to thank God and to tell others when He answers your prayers.

Use the spaces on the prayer pages to draw pictures or write the names of special people you want to pray for. Don't forget to include the things for which you are thankful.

Things You Need for Your Quiet Time

Your Bible

Your Quiet Time

Crayons

A Pencil

A Quiet Place

5

Christian Service Activities

The following activities are for you to accomplish with your child to help them develop selflessness and a Christ-like concern for others. These activities can also be used for family enrichment.

1. Goodness Basket: You will need: the ingredients for your favorite cookies. Bake cookies with your child and take them to someone you know who is a shut-in, or has a special need. This is teaching your child to help others who are alone.

Date Completed: _____ **Initials:** _____

2. Love Coupons: You will need: paper, markers or crayons, stickers, scissors, and stapler. Have your child think of *helping jobs* that he or she can do for someone else. Work together to design coupons with these jobs on them. Have your child give the coupons to people and then perform the task for them when asked.

Date Completed: _____ **Initials:** _____

3. Special Messages: You will need: paper, stickers, markers or crayons, and a treat. Make special notes with your child to give to people who need encouragement. Deliver them with a smile and a little treat to make it extra special. Be a messenger of kindness to someone else.

Date Completed: _____ **Initials:** _____

4. Tracts: You will need: colored paper, markers or crayons, and stickers. Make a tract from the colored paper. Help your child write the story of Jesus. Write in the tract "Jesus loves you," "Jesus Died for you," and "Will you ask Him to be your Savior today?" Give this to someone this week.

Date Completed: _____ **Initials:** _____

5. Act out a Bible Story: You will need: Bible costumes or paper, markers or crayons. As you read a story from the Bible, involve the whole family in acting out the story. Or help your child draw pictures of the story and allow him or her to tell the story to the family.

Date Completed: _____ **Initials:** _____

6. Gospel Bracelets or Necklaces: You will need: black, red, white, green, and yellow beads, cording, and scissors. Cut the cording to fit your child's wrist for a bracelet or to fit around the neck for a necklace. String the beads onto the cording using the pattern below to represent the Gospel message. Use this as a tool to tell others of our living, risen Savior.

Beads: Yellow = God's love for us, John 3:16;
  Black = sin, Romans 3:23;
  Red = blood, Hebrews 9:22;
  White = forgiveness, John 1:12;
  Green = growing in the Lord, 1 John 1:9.

Date Completed: _____   Initials: _____

7. Kindness Basket: You will need: a container of some sort (basket), and blessing items. God wants us to be busy doing things for others. Make a kindness basket with your child for someone who needs encouragement. Include items to make it a blessing (food, notes, flowers, candles, pictures, etc.); make it extra special and then have your child deliver it to the person with a smile.

Date Completed: _____   Initials: _____

8. Share a Treat: You will need: the ingredients to make your child's favorite snack. Make the snack with your child and have your child share it with a friend. This helps your child to learn compassion and kindness to others.

Date Completed: _____   Initials: _____

9. Planting flowers: You will need: a flower pot, soil (dirt), water, trowel, and seeds. Plant the seed that your child chooses. The back of most seed packets will contain specific instructions for that particular flower. Remind the child that we can plant the seed and water the seed, but only God will cause the seed to grow.

Date Completed: _____   Initials: _____

10. Thank You Note: You will need: supplies to create a card (glitter, paint, stickers, magazine pictures, picture of child, etc.), paper, scissors, glue, and markers or crayons. Help your child write a thank you note to a teacher or a leader who has helped him or her learn God's Word. Be creative and deliver it in a special way!

Date Completed: _____   Initials: _____

11. Personal Bible Storybook: You will need: construction paper, glitter, pictures, paint, stickers, markers or crayons, glue, and stapler. Help your child draw pictures to illustrate his or her three favorite Bible stories. Decorate a piece of construction paper to create a cover for the book. Using another piece of construction paper as a back cover, staple the pictures and covers together. Your child now has his or her own Bible storybook that they can use to tell other people about the Bible!

Date Completed: _____   Initials: _____

12. Wordless Bookmark: You will need: scissors, paper, construction paper (black, red, white, yellow and green), glue, markers or crayons, and clear contact paper or shipping tape. Help your child cut a piece of plain paper the desired size of bookmark. Mark the paper into five even sections. Cut a piece of yellow, black, red, white, and green construction paper the size of the previous marked off sections. Glue the colors onto the bookmark in the order they were listed above. On the back of the bookmark write the key:
Yellow = God's love for us, John 3:16;
Black = sin, Romans 3:23;
Red = blood, Hebrews 9:22;
White = forgiveness, John 1:12;
Green = growing in the Lord, 1 John 1:9.

To ensure a long-life for the bookmark, cover it with clear contact paper or clear shipping tape.

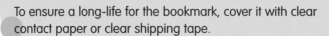

Date Completed: _____   Initials: _____

My Prayer Diary

These pages are where you can draw a picture or write words to remind you to pray for special people or things that you care about.

My Prayer Diary

My Prayer Diary

My Prayer Diary

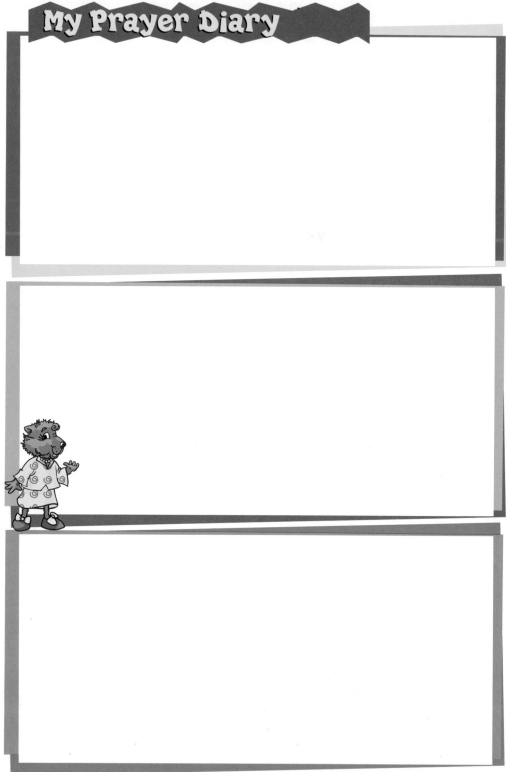

SUNDAY

I CAN KNOW

God will bless you for loving and obeying His Word, the Bible. You will be like a tree that gets plenty of sunshine and water. A tree that gets plenty of sunshine and water is very strong and always has good fruit on it.

I CAN LEARN

Draw a ⭕ around how many in each row.

4   5   6

4   5   6

4   5   6

4   5   6

I CAN PRAY

WEEK #1

Ask God to help you show others you love Him by your good actions.

13

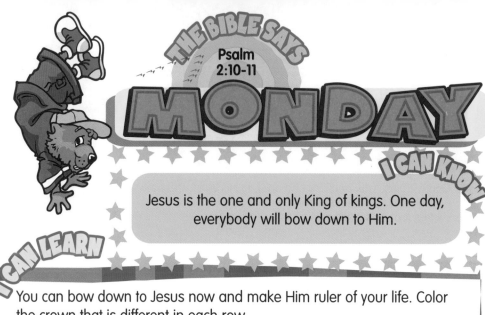

I CAN KNOW

Jesus is the one and only King of kings. One day, everybody will bow down to Him.

I CAN LEARN

You can bow down to Jesus now and make Him ruler of your life. Color the crown that is different in each row.

I CAN PRAY

WEEK #1

Ask God to help you let Him rule your life.

14

5 5 5

TUESDAY

I CAN KNOW

You don't need to be afraid. God is watching over you, even when you're asleep.

I CAN LEARN

God is always watching over you. How many of these can you find in the picture? Write the number in the box.

I CAN PRAY

Ask God to help you not to be afraid.

WEEK #1

15

WEDNESDAY

I CAN KNOW

God will give you more joy than anything here on earth.

I CAN LEARN

When you obey God, He gives you gladness and peace. Half of these pictures are missing. Draw the other half. Then color the pictures.

I CAN PRAY

Thank God for giving you a joyful heart.

WEEK #1

16

God hears you when you pray. He will listen to you no matter where you are or what time of day it is.

I CAN LEARN

You can pray anytime and anywhere. Find the words morning, noon and night in the puzzle and circle them.

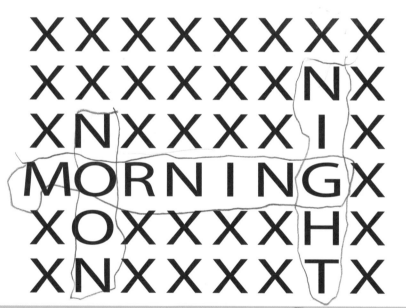

```
X X X X X X X X X
X X X X X X X N X
X N X X X X X I X
M O R N I N G X
X O X X X X X H X
X N X X X X T X
```

MORNING   NOON   NIGHT

I CAN PRAY

WEEK #1

Tell God thank you for listening to you when you pray.

THE BIBLE SAYS
Psalm 6:9

FRIDAY

I CAN KNOW

King David talked to God about his problems. He knew that God would take care of him.

I CAN LEARN

God wants you to talk to Him about your problems. Color the picture that shows what you should do when someone is unkind to you.

I CAN PRAY

WEEK #1

Pray for someone who has been unkind to you.

18

SATURDAY

THE BIBLE SAYS
Psalm 7:1

I CAN KNOW

You can ask God for help. Nothing is too hard for Him.

I CAN LEARN

Draw a ⭕ around what you need God's help with. Draw an ✖ over the things that you already know how to do.

WAY TO GO!

I CAN PRAY

Ask God to help you obey and be kind to others.

WEEK #1

I CAN KNOW

Obeying God makes you happy. Disobeying makes you sad.

I CAN LEARN

Draw a ———— to match the picture to the correct face.

I CAN PRAY

Ask God to help you obey your parents with a happy heart.

WEEK #2

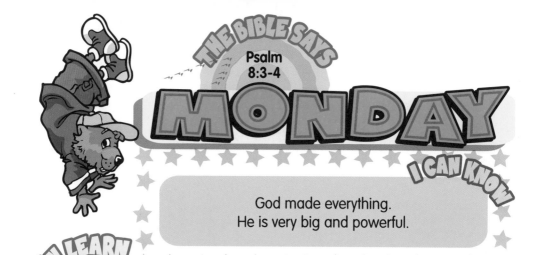

God made everything.
He is very big and powerful.

I CAN LEARN

God loves you very much. Write the missing number on the line.

I CAN PRAY

Tell God thank you for being so powerful.

WEEK #2

21

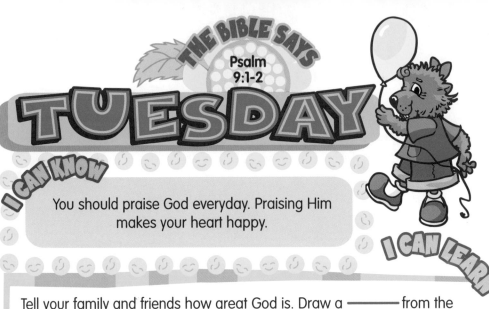

THE BIBLE SAYS
Psalm 9:1-2
TUESDAY

You should praise God everyday. Praising Him makes your heart happy.

I CAN LEARN

Tell your family and friends how great God is. Draw a ———— from the children to the word Happy.

HAPPY

I CAN PRAY

WEEK #2

Praise God for something special He has done.

22

THE BIBLE SAYS
Psalm 9:19-20

WEDNESDAY

I CAN KNOW

God sees everyone and everything. You can't hide from Him.

I CAN LEARN

Color the empty spaces black and the dotted spaces yellow to find out who can't hide from God.

I CAN PRAY

WEEK #2

Pray for someone you know who needs to know about Jesus.

23

I CAN KNOW

There is no way to be truly happy without God. The only way you can have peace and joy is by loving and obeying Him.

I CAN LEARN

What face would you make? Draw a ◯ around the words happy or sad.

happy   sad

happy   sad

happy   sad

I CAN PRAY

Tell God how much you love Him.

WEEK #2

FRIDAY

I CAN KNOW

God promises to be a Father to
you and to protect you.

I CAN LEARN

God hears you when you call for help. Draw a ⬭ around the 4 things
in the bottom picture that are different.

I CAN PRAY

Tell God thank you for hearing you when you pray.

WEEK #2

25

I CAN KNOW

God will forgive you when you do wrong. All you have to do is ask Him.

I CAN LEARN

Jesus is always ready with open arms to welcome you. Start at 2. Connect the dots counting by twos from 2 to 20.

WAY TO GO!

I CAN PRAY

Ask God to forgive you for something you've done wrong.

WEEK #2

26

I CAN KNOW

God is good, and He will always do what is best for you.

I CAN LEARN

Draw a picture of something good God has given you.

I CAN PRAY

WEEK #3

Tell God thank you for the good things He gives you.

27

I CAN KNOW

God will always love you. Singing is a wonderful way to praise Him for His great love.

I CAN LEARN

Sing the song "Jesus Loves Me." Draw the musical note to finish each pattern. Make your own pattern in the last row.

I CAN PRAY

Tell God thank you for His love for you.

WEEK #3

28

THE BIBLE SAYS

Psalm 14:2-3

TUESDAY

Without Jesus, you cannot do anything good.
There is no one who does good, except Jesus.

I CAN LEARN

Jesus is the One who helps you do good things. Good starts with the beginning sound g. Draw a ———— from the letter G to the pictures that begin with the letter sound G.

Gg

I CAN PRAY

WEEK #3

Ask Jesus to help you do good things.

29

THE BIBLE SAYS
Psalm 15:1-2

WEDNESDAY

I CAN KNOW

Lying and disobeying are sins. You can please God by doing what is right and speaking the truth.

I CAN LEARN

God is happy when you speak the truth. Follow the smiley faces. Color them red. Where do they lead?

START HERE!

TRUTH

I CAN PRAY

WEEK #3

Ask God to help you tell the truth.

30

THURSDAY

I CAN KNOW

God will give you a glad heart and a song to sing when you fill your mind with His Word.

I CAN LEARN

If you are a child of God, He will never leave you. Draw your right hand in the space. Trace the word Right.

Right

I CAN PRAY

Tell God thank you for always being with you.

WEEK #3

31

THE BIBLE SAYS

Psalm 17:5

FRIDAY

I CAN KNOW

Obeying God will keep you on the right path. Just follow Him. He knows the way.

I CAN LEARN

Color the 👣's that take you to Jesus. He's leading the way.

I CAN PRAY

Ask Jesus to lead you in everything you do.

WEEK #3

THE BIBLE SAYS

Psalm 17:15

SATURDAY

I CAN KNOW

When you obey God's Word, the Bible, you act more like Jesus.

I CAN LEARN

Whom should you be like? Trace the picture in the mirror to see Who you should act like.

WAY TO GO!

WEEK #3

I CAN PRAY

Pray that you will show what Jesus is like to others.

33

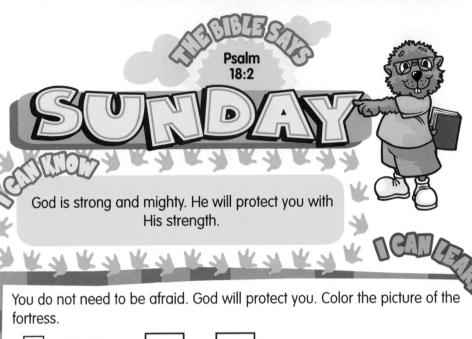

I CAN KNOW

God is strong and mighty. He will protect you with His strength.

I CAN LEARN

You do not need to be afraid. God will protect you. Color the picture of the fortress.

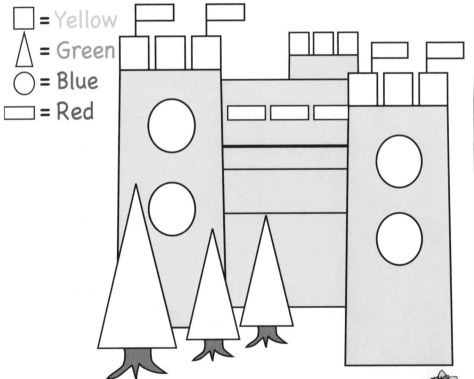

☐ = Yellow

△ = Green

○ = Blue

▭ = Red

I CAN PRAY

WEEK #4

Ask God to protect you and your family.

34

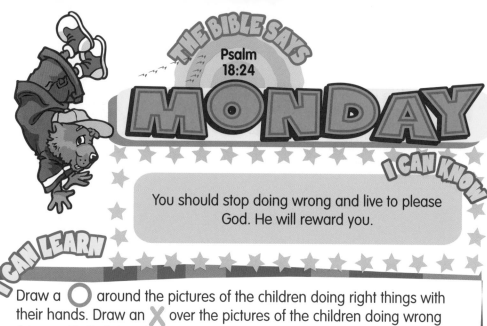

I CAN KNOW

You should stop doing wrong and live to please God. He will reward you.

I CAN LEARN

Draw a ⭕ around the pictures of the children doing right things with their hands. Draw an ✗ over the pictures of the children doing wrong things with their hands.

I CAN PRAY

Ask God to help you do what is right.

WEEK #4

35

TUESDAY

THE BIBLE SAYS
Psalm 18:28

I CAN KNOW

God is light. He can turn all darkness and sin to goodness and light.

I CAN LEARN

Draw a ⭕ around all the pictures that give light.

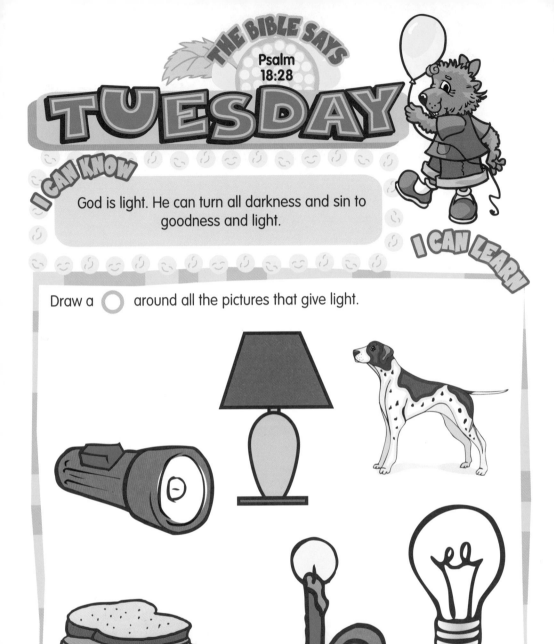

I CAN PRAY

Pray for someone who is sick.

WEEK #4

36

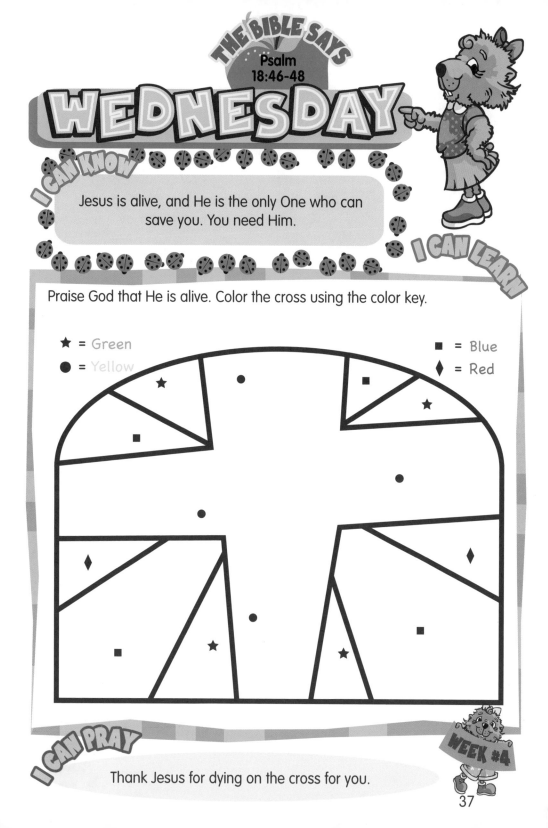

I CAN KNOW

Jesus is alive, and He is the only One who can save you. You need Him.

I CAN LEARN

Praise God that He is alive. Color the cross using the color key.

★ = Green
● = Yellow
■ = Blue
♦ = Red

I CAN PRAY

WEEK #4

Thank Jesus for dying on the cross for you.

37

Psalm
19:7-8

THURSDAY

I CAN KNOW

The Bible shows you how to live. Obeying God's
Word will give you peace and joy.

I CAN LEARN

Draw a ——— from A to H to show you what you need to read everyday.

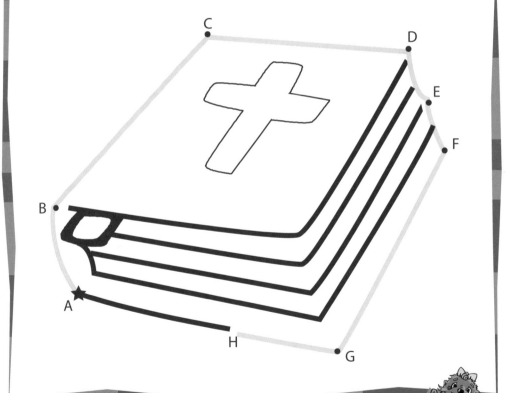

I CAN PRAY

Tell God thank you for the Bible.

WEEK #4

THE BIBLE SAYS
Psalm 20:7

FRIDAY

You should only put your trust in God. He will take care of you.

You can believe God's promises. Trace the letters so you can find out who you should trust.

Trust only
in the Lord our

God.

WEEK #4

Ask God to help you trust Him.

Psalm 21:13

SATURDAY

I CAN KNOW

Praising shows God that you love Him. You can praise Him with a song or prayer.

I CAN LEARN

Circle the words in the puzzle that show how you can praise God.

```
X   X   X   P   X
S   H   A   R   E
I   X   X   A   X
N   X   X   Y   X
X   X   X   X   X
G   I   V   E   X
```

WAY TO GO!

I CAN PRAY

Tell God how much you love Him.

WEEK #4

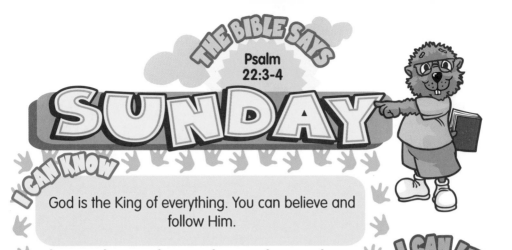

I CAN KNOW

God is the King of everything. You can believe and follow Him.

I CAN LEARN

These crowns can remind you that God is the King. Write the missing number.

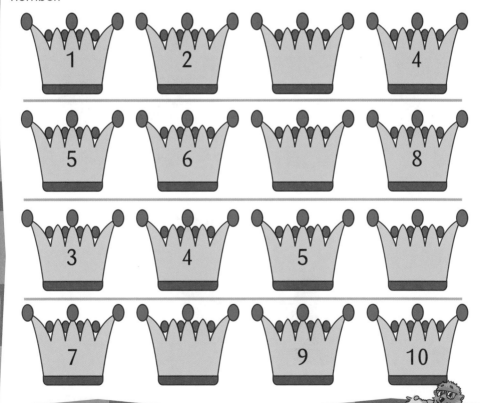

I CAN PRAY

Ask God to help you follow Him.

WEEK #5

41

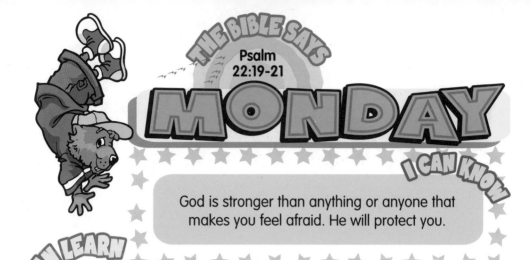

God is stronger than anything or anyone that makes you feel afraid. He will protect you.

I CAN LEARN

Draw a ⬭ around the things you need to trust God for.

I CAN PRAY

WEEK #5

Ask God to help you not be afraid.

42

TUESDAY

I CAN KNOW

God gives you good things. He deserves your praise and worship. You should thank Him for His goodness to you.

I CAN LEARN

God gives you good food to eat. Look at the chart and answer the questions.

 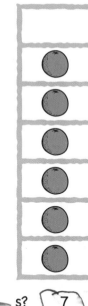 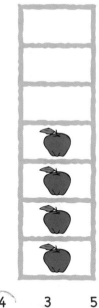

How many s?	7	4	3	5
How many s?	6	3	5	7
How many s?	4	6	2	5

I CAN PRAY

Thank God for the good food He gives you.

THE BIBLE SAYS
Psalm 23:1-6

WEDNESDAY

I CAN KNOW

God takes care of you the way a good shepherd cares for his sheep. He will make sure you have all you need.

I CAN LEARN

Draw a line to help the shepherd find his lost sheep.

Go to the ▬ .
Turn and go to the ▲ .
Turn and go to the ■ .
Go straight to the 🐑 .

I CAN PRAY

Tell God thank you for taking good care of you.

WEEK #5

44

Psalm 24:1-2

THURSDAY

I CAN KNOW

God made the world and everything that is in it.
Even you were made by God.

I CAN LEARN

Here are some things that God made. What letter begins each picture name? Circle the upper and lowercase letters.

 Ee   E   e   C

 Ff   d   f   F

 Tt   T   b   t

 Dd   b   D   d

I CAN PRAY

Thank God for making you.

WEEK #5

45

FRIDAY

God has a special path He wants you to follow. He will show you the way in His Word, the Bible.

God's direction book for your life is the Bible. Write the letter on the path that matches the key.

= B

= E

= I

= L

WEEK #5

Ask God to help you follow Him.

Psalm 25:16-17

SATURDAY

Only Jesus can forgive your sin and fill the sad, lonely places of your life.

If you have sin in your life ask Jesus to forgive you. He will. Write the first letter of each object in the box to read the message.

WAY TO GO!

Ask Jesus to help you not feel sad.

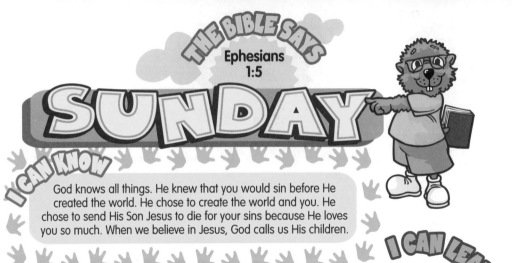

I CAN KNOW

God knows all things. He knew that you would sin before He created the world. He chose to create the world and you. He chose to send His Son Jesus to die for your sins because He loves you so much. When we believe in Jesus, God calls us His children.

I CAN LEARN

Color the picture of Jesus and His family. Are you part of His family? Talk to your parents or an adult at church if you are not sure.

I CAN PRAY

Thank God for His great love for you.

WEEK #6

48

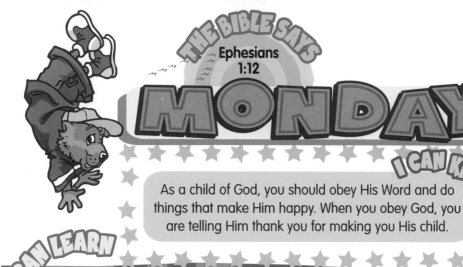

As a child of God, you should obey His Word and do things that make Him happy. When you obey God, you are telling Him thank you for making you His child.

I CAN LEARN

Write the beginning letter sounds on the lines to spell out what your good actions say to God.

I CAN PRAY

Ask God to help you do things that make Him happy.

WEEK #6

49

THE BIBLE SAYS
Ephesians 1:19

TUESDAY

God has great power and mighty strength. He shares this with us, so we can do great things for Him.

Power begins with the beginning sound P. Draw a ⬤ around the pictures that begin with the letter sound P. Write the letters P and p in the blanks.

Thank God for giving you strength to do good things when you ask Him.

WEEK #6

50

WEDNESDAY

I CAN KNOW

God is kind, forgiving and loving. He wanted to save you from your sin even before you knew Him.

I CAN LEARN

Draw a line from 1 to 12. Trace the letters written on the cross to see what God says to you.

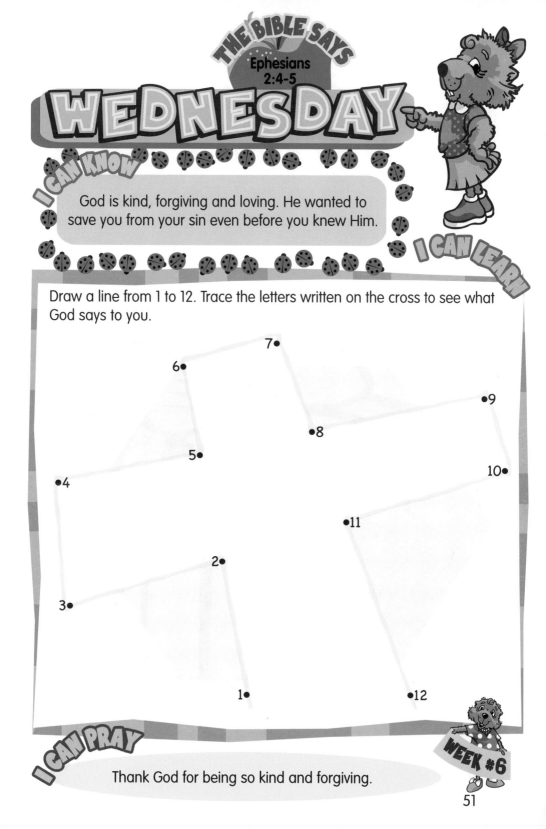

I CAN PRAY

Thank God for being so kind and forgiving.

WEEK #6

51

By believing that Jesus died for your sins, God saves you from your sin. It is His gift to you. You have to accept the gift from Him. You cannot work to earn the gift. He wants to just give it to you.

I CAN LEARN

Jesus gave you the free gift of salvation. Use the color code to color the picture.

1=Yellow
2= Blue
3= Red

I CAN PRAY

Thank God for His free gift of salvation.

WEEK #6

Ephesians 2:18

FRIDAY

I CAN KNOW

You can pray to God without having to have someone else pray for you. You can pray to God anytime you want.

I CAN LEARN

These children are praying at different times of the day. Write 1, 2 and 3 to show the order.

I CAN PRAY

Tell God thank you for always listening when you pray.

WEEK #6

THE BIBLE SAYS

Ephesians 2:19

SATURDAY

When you ask Jesus to save you from your sin, you are part of God's family and no longer a stranger to God.

I CAN LEARN

Others who are saved are your brothers and sisters in Christ. We are all family.
Follow the path that a child of God takes once he is saved and becomes part of God's family.

WAY TO GO!

WEEK #6

I CAN PRAY

Ask God to bless your church, your Christian friends and family.

54

Ephesians 3:7

SUNDAY

Paul went to different places telling about God
because God had given him the gift of teaching.
God wants all of us to tell others about Him.

I CAN LEARN

Solve the riddles to draw in the missing parts.

You use your mouth to tell others about God.

Others use their ears to hear you.

I CAN PRAY

WEEK #7

Ask God to help you be brave and tell others about Him.

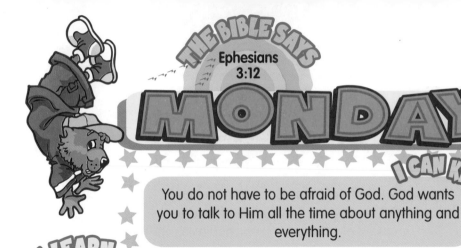

THE BIBLE SAYS
Ephesians 3:12

MONDAY

I CAN KNOW

You do not have to be afraid of God. God wants you to talk to Him all the time about anything and everything.

I CAN LEARN

Draw a ⭕ around the 5 hidden praying hands in the picture. Write the number 5 in the box.

I CAN PRAY

Thank God for listening when you pray.

WEEK #7

56

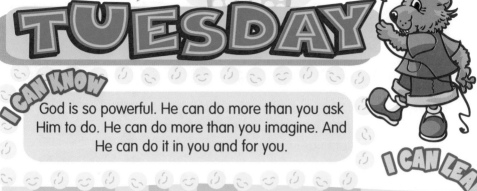

TUESDAY

THE BIBLE SAYS

Ephesians 3:20

I CAN KNOW

God is so powerful. He can do more than you ask Him to do. He can do more than you imagine. And He can do it in you and for you.

I CAN LEARN

Hold your book in front of a mirror to read the secret message. Who gives you power?

boƆ

I CAN PRAY

Praise God for His power.

WEEK #7

WEDNESDAY

I CAN KNOW

God wants you to be at peace with others. You need to try your hardest not to fight with others, but to get along.

I CAN LEARN

Peace starts with the beginning letter sound P. Fight starts with the beginning letter sound F. Draw a ——— from each picture to the word it belongs with.

Peace

Fight

I CAN PRAY

WEEK #7

Ask God to help you not fight, but get along with others.

THURSDAY

I CAN KNOW

You always need to tell the truth, but God wants you to speak kindly and lovingly to others. When you speak nicely, you are being careful not to hurt someone's feelings.

I CAN LEARN

Draw an X over the picture that does not belong with others.

I CAN PRAY

Ask God to help you tell the truth always and to speak nicely.

WEEK #7

59

THE BIBLE SAYS
Ephesians 4:24

FRIDAY

When you ask Jesus to be your Savior, you need to live as God wants you to. Sometimes this means not doing the things you want to do or the things others are doing.

When you obey God's Word, the Bible, you will live like God wants you to. Draw a line to what God wants you to do.

I can do anything I want to.

Start ▶

I need to obey God's Word.

Ask God to help you be strong and do only what He wants you to do.

WEEK #7

60

You need to be kind to others and forgive others when they hurt you. Jesus did this for you, so you need to do it for others.

I CAN LEARN

The word kind begins with the letter sound k. Draw a line from the word kind to the pictures that begin with the letter sound k. Trace the word kind.

WAY TO GO!

WEEK #7

I CAN PRAY

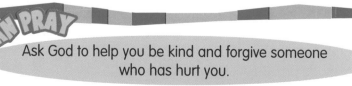

Ask God to help you be kind and forgive someone who has hurt you.

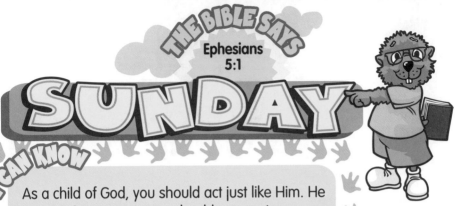

I CAN KNOW

As a child of God, you should act just like Him. He is someone you should copy cat.

I CAN LEARN

Draw a circle around the child who is copying the first child.

I CAN PRAY

Ask God to help you be like Him in the things you do and the things you say.

WEEK #8

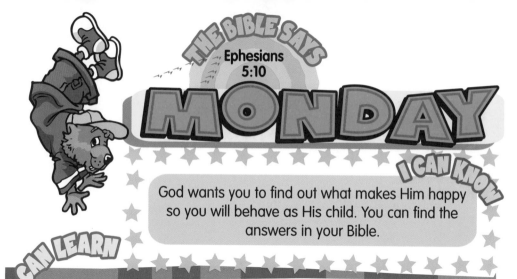

I CAN KNOW

God wants you to find out what makes Him happy so you will behave as His child. You can find the answers in your Bible.

I CAN LEARN

Color in the happy face next to the picture if it makes God happy. If it doesn't, color in the sad face.

I CAN PRAY

Ask God to help you learn what pleases Him.

WEEK #8

63

THE BIBLE SAYS

Ephesians 5:20

TUESDAY

You should always give thanks to God for everything.

Write the beginning letter sound of each picture.

WEEK #8

Tell God thank you for 3 things He has given you.

64

WEDNESDAY

God wants husbands and wives to love and respect each other. They need to love each other more than they love themselves.

Color the heart to finish the color pattern.

WEEK #8

Pray for your dad and mom today.

God's Word, the Bible, tells you to obey your parents because it is the right thing to do. It will please God. To obey means to listen and do what your parents ask you the first time.

I CAN LEARN

Draw a line from the sentence to the picture that matches it.

I will go to bed when I am told to.

I will pick up my toys when I am told to.

I CAN PRAY

WEEK #8

Ask God to help you obey your parents all the time.

FRIDAY

I CAN KNOW

By reading and learning God's Word, the Bible, you are like a solider putting on your armor. Your armor protects you from harm. Knowing God's Word will help you say no to sin and be strong for God.

I CAN LEARN

Help this soldier get dressed for battle. Draw a line from each piece of armor to where it belongs.

I CAN PRAY

Thank God for His Word and ask Him to help you remember it so you can be strong for Him.

WEEK #8

You can pray everywhere, for everything, and ask God for anything. God wants you to do that. He also wants you to pray for others who believe in Jesus.

I CAN LEARN

Pray begins with the letter sound P. Draw a ◯ around the pictures that begin with the letter P. Trace the word Pray.

Pray

WAY TO GO!

WEEK #8

THE BIBLE SAYS

Esther 1:12

SUNDAY

I CAN KNOW

King Xerxes threw a big party to show how great he was. He wanted to show off his wife, Queen Vashti, to his friends. The king became angry when his wife wouldn't come to his party.

I CAN LEARN

God does not want you to show off your toys and other things that He has given you. Say the picture words. Circle the picture word that begins with the same sound.

Queen	Quilt	Ball

King	Bike	Kite

I CAN PRAY

WEEK #9

Tell God thank you for the things He has given to you.

69

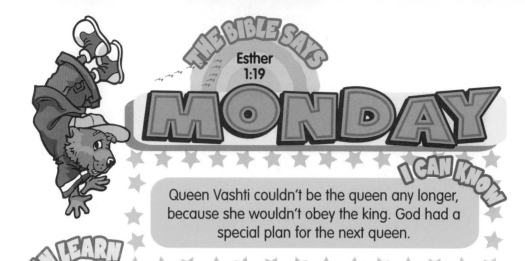

Esther 1:19

MONDAY

THE BIBLE SAYS

Queen Vashti couldn't be the queen any longer, because she wouldn't obey the king. God had a special plan for the next queen.

I CAN LEARN

God has a plan for you, too. Draw an X over the crown that doesn't belong in each row.

I CAN PRAY

Tell God thank you for the special plan He has for you.

WEEK #9

70

I CAN KNOW

Mordecai took care of his cousin, Esther. He showed love and kindness for Esther. You should show love for others.

I CAN LEARN

Draw a ☐ around the pictures of the children who are showing love to others.

I CAN PRAY

Ask God to help you show kindness to a friend.

WEEK #9

THE BIBLE SAYS
Esther 2:17-18

WEDNESDAY

I CAN KNOW

Esther was a young lady that God was going to use to help His people, the Israelites.

I CAN LEARN

God wants you to help others, too. Draw a line from the pictures on the left to a picture on the right to show how the children can help others.

I CAN PRAY

WEEK #9

Ask God to show you someone who needs your help.

Mordecai would not bow to evil Haman. He knew he should only bow down and worship God.

I CAN LEARN

Trace the letters to spell who you should worship.

God

I CAN PRAY

Praise God for being so wonderful!

WEEK #9

THE BIBLE SAYS
Esther 4:15-16

FRIDAY

I CAN KNOW

Esther asked the people to pray for her. She knew she needed God's help.

I CAN LEARN

Prayer begins with the letter sound P. Trace the letter P. Draw a ——— from the word pictures that begin with the letter sound P to the letter P.

I CAN PRAY

Pray for your parents.

WEEK #9

74

I CAN KNOW

Queen Esther invited the king and Haman to dinner. She was going to tell the king about Haman's evil plan. God had a special plan for Esther to save the Jews from Haman's evil plan.

God has a special plan for your life, too. Draw a ——— from 1 to 10. Say the numbers out loud as you draw. Color the food on the plate. Trace the pictures of the knife, fork and spoon.

WAY
TO GO!

WEEK #9

Tell God thank you for the special plan He has for your life.

Esther 6:10

SUNDAY

The king wanted to reward Mordecai for saving his life. Haman thought the king wanted to reward him. His pride got him in a lot of trouble.

Pride is thinking too much about yourself. God wants you to put others first. Draw a line to match the opposites.

WEEK #10

Ask God to help you think of others before yourself.

76

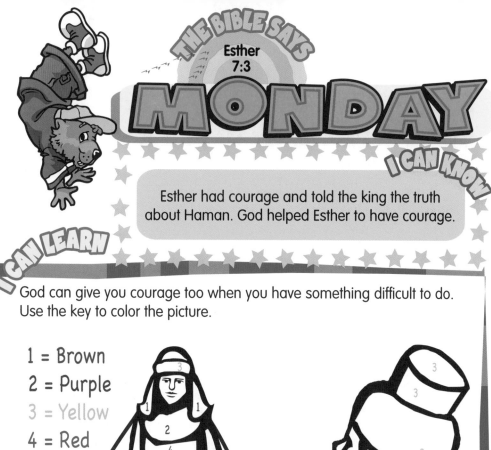

THE BIBLE SAYS

MONDAY

Esther 7:3

Esther had courage and told the king the truth about Haman. God helped Esther to have courage.

I CAN LEARN

God can give you courage too when you have something difficult to do. Use the key to color the picture.

1 = Brown
2 = Purple
3 = Yellow
4 = Red

I CAN PRAY

Ask God to help you have courage.

WEEK #10

Esther 8:15-16

TUESDAY

I CAN KNOW

The king took all that belonged to Haman and gave it to Mordecai. Esther and Mordecai obeyed God, and He gave them courage.

I CAN LEARN

You can do the right thing even if you're the only one. Some things come in pairs, and others stand alone. Draw a ◯ around the objects that don't need a match.

I CAN PRAY

Ask God to help you do what is right.

WEEK #10

WEDNESDAY

I CAN KNOW

Mordecai was now working with the king. He helped the Jewish people to be safe.

I CAN LEARN

Mordecai starts with the letter sound M. Color the pictures that begin with the letter sound M.

I CAN PRAY

Tell God thank you for keeping you safe.

WEEK #10

79

Esther 9:22

THURSDAY

I CAN KNOW

Mordecai told all the Jews to celebrate because of the great victory God had given them.

I CAN LEARN

You should praise God for all He has done for you. Find the hidden pictures, and draw a ◯ around them.

I CAN PRAY

Praise God for your mom and dad.

WEEK #10

I CAN KNOW

God created a beautiful world for you to enjoy. He really loves you.

I CAN LEARN

Draw a picture of your favorite animal, flower or insect. Trace the letters to remind you who made this world.

I CAN PRAY

Thank God for His creation.

WEEK #10

81

THE BIBLE SAYS

Song of Solomon 6:3

SATURDAY

I CAN KNOW

Marriage is a beautiful gift from God. Husbands and wives are to love each other for the rest of their lives.

I CAN LEARN

Color the next one.

WAY TO GO!

I CAN PRAY

Ask God to help you show love to someone today.

WEEK #10

82

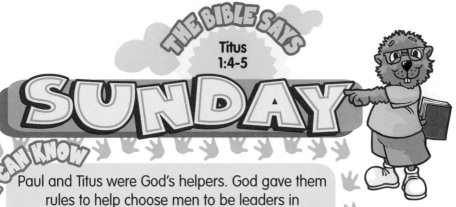

I CAN KNOW

Paul and Titus were God's helpers. God gave them rules to help choose men to be leaders in the church.

I CAN LEARN

What can you do today to show that you want to be God's special helper? Use the key to color the letters. Write the word on the line.

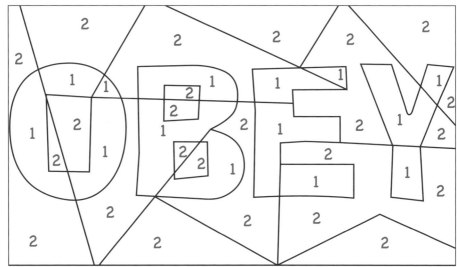

1 = Red
2 = Blue

I CAN PRAY

Pray for the leaders in your church.

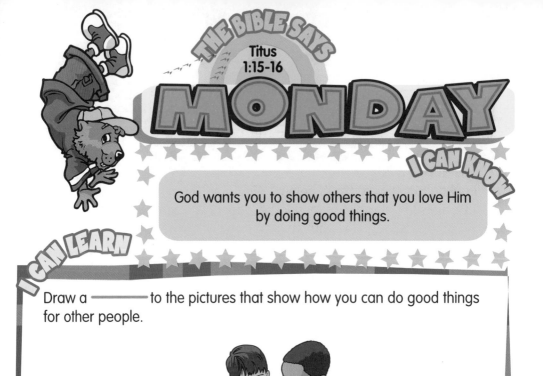

God wants you to show others that you love Him by doing good things.

Draw a ———— to the pictures that show how you can do good things for other people.

Ask God to help you do good things for others.

WEEK #11

I CAN KNOW

You need to be a good example to others by obeying God.

I CAN LEARN

Draw a ——————— from 2 to 20 to show who you need to obey.

14• •16
•18
12• •20
10• 6•
8• 4•
2•

I CAN PRAY

Ask God to help you be a good example to others.

WEEK #11

85

THE BIBLE SAYS
Titus 2:11-13

WEDNESDAY

I CAN KNOW

When you have Jesus as your Savior, you need to make the right choices. You need to say NO to things that would not please God.

I CAN LEARN

The children in these pictures are making different choices. Draw a ⃝ around the word Yes or No under the picture.

Are they choosing to obey God?

Yes   No   Yes   No

Yes   No   Yes   No

I CAN PRAY

Ask God to help you make the choices that would please Him.

WEEK #11

86

When you become God's child, He forgives ALL your sin and gives you eternal life. That means you will live with Him forever.

I CAN LEARN

Forever begins with the letter sound F. Draw a ——— from the letter F to the picture that has the beginning sound F. Write the letter F on the line.

Ff

I CAN PRAY

Tell God thank you for sending His Son, Jesus, to forgive your sin.

WEEK #11

87

FRIDAY

Philemon invited people who loved Jesus to his home. This is called hospitality.

When you have visitors in your home, you should treat them kindly. Color the house.

☐ = red.

△ = green.

◯ = yellow.

☐ = blue.

WEEK #11

Ask God to help you be kind to visitors in your home.

88

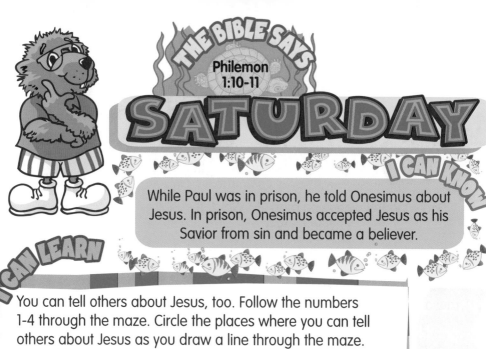

While Paul was in prison, he told Onesimus about Jesus. In prison, Onesimus accepted Jesus as his Savior from sin and became a believer.

I CAN LEARN

You can tell others about Jesus, too. Follow the numbers 1-4 through the maze. Circle the places where you can tell others about Jesus as you draw a line through the maze.

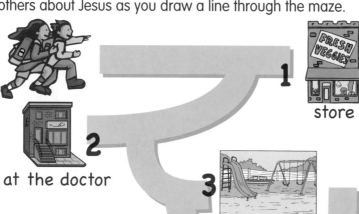

1 store

2 at the doctor

3 park

4 in my neighborhood

Tell others about Jesus.

WAY TO GO!

WEEK #11

I CAN PRAY

Ask God to help you share Jesus with others.

89

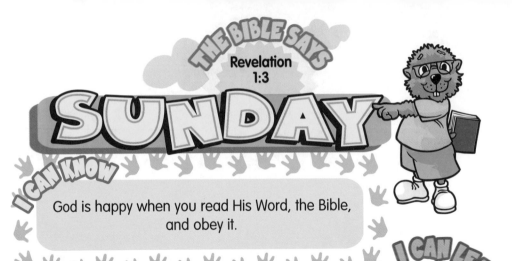

I CAN KNOW

God is happy when you read His Word, the Bible, and obey it.

I CAN LEARN

Draw a line from 2 to 20 so you know what you need to read and obey.

6 •

8 •

10 •

12 •

14 •

16 •

4 •

Bible

★ 2

20 •

18 •

I CAN PRAY

WEEK #12

Ask God to help you obey His Word.

I CAN KNOW

John was sent to the island of Patmos because he was telling others The Good News of Jesus.

I CAN LEARN

If you were sent to an island and you could not take any of your family or friends, what would you take with you? Color the islands **yellow** that have something on them that you would take with you.

I CAN PRAY

WEEK #12

Ask God for a chance to tell someone about Jesus.

THE BIBLE SAYS

Revelation 1:18-19

TUESDAY

Jesus is alive and you can live forever, too, if you ask Jesus to be your Savior from your sin.

If Jesus is your Savior, you will live with Him forever in heaven. Draw a picture of yourself standing next to Jesus.

WEEK #12

Thank Jesus that you can know Him.

WEDNESDAY

I CAN KNOW

Jesus wants you to love Him most. You can show Jesus you love Him most by obeying Him.

I CAN LEARN

◯ the number of hearts in each row. Color the hearts.

1　2　3　4　5

1　2　3　4　5

1　2　3　4　5

1　2　3　4　5

I CAN PRAY

WEEK #12

Ask God to help you love Jesus most.

When you are faithful to Jesus, He will give you a crown in heaven.

I CAN LEARN

You are faithful to Jesus when you obey Him. Draw a ——— from each crown to its shadow. Color the jewels in the crowns.

I CAN PRAY

Ask Jesus to help you be faithful.

WEEK #12

FRIDAY

I CAN KNOW

Jesus knows where you live and what you are doing all the time.

I CAN LEARN

You cannot hide anything from Jesus. Find the eyes in the picture and color them. Write how many you found.

I CAN PRAY

Tell Jesus thank you for always watching you.

WEEK #12

I CAN KNOW

Jesus wants you to obey the Bible. When you obey Jesus, you will always be a winner.

I CAN LEARN

Draw a ——— to help the children find how to be winners.

Obey God.

WAY TO GO!

I CAN PRAY

Ask God to help you be a good listener of His Word, the Bible.

WEEK #12

96

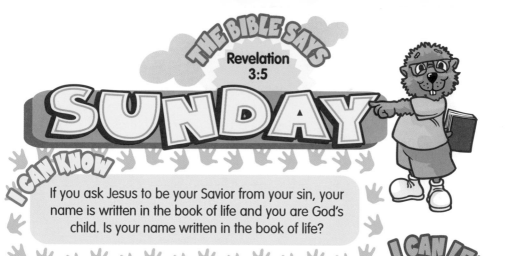

THE BIBLE SAYS

Revelation 3:5

SUNDAY

If you ask Jesus to be your Savior from your sin, your name is written in the book of life and you are God's child. Is your name written in the book of life?

I CAN LEARN

Has Jesus written your name in the book of life? Draw a ———— under the biggest one.

I CAN PRAY

WEEK #13

Tell Jesus thank you for saving you and writing your name in the book of life.

THE BIBLE SAYS

Revelation 3:7-8

MONDAY

I CAN KNOW

Jesus has the keys to heaven. He is the only One who can open and shut the doors to heaven.

I CAN LEARN

If you have asked Jesus to be your Savior, then He will open the door to heaven for you. Match the key to the door it will open.

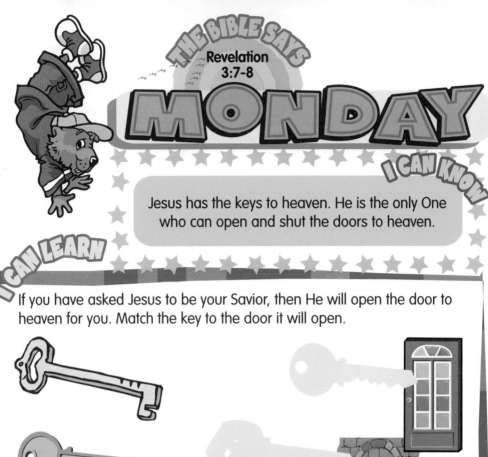

I CAN PRAY

Thank Jesus for opening the door to heaven to you.

WEEK #13

98

TUESDAY

THE BIBLE SAYS
Revelation 3:20-21

I CAN KNOW

Jesus wants to have a friendship with you. He talks to you through the Bible, and you talk to Him through prayer.

I CAN LEARN

Draw a around the picture of how Jesus talks to you.

I CAN PRAY

WEEK #13

Thank Jesus for your special friendship with Him.

99

I CAN KNOW

God deserves our praise. He is the Creator of everything. You should praise God because He is the Creator.

I CAN LEARN

Look at some of the things that God created. Count how many.

frogs	4	1	3
ducks	6	5	4
mice	3	4	2
butterflies	2	5	4
children	3	6	5

I CAN PRAY

WEEK #13

Tell God something you love about Him.

I CAN KNOW

A scroll is like a book, but it rolls up. This scroll was sealed seven times. Jesus is the only one who is able to open the scroll.

I CAN LEARN

Fill in the missing numbers.

2

6

I CAN PRAY

Tell Jesus thank you for being mighty.

WEEK #13

FRIDAY

I CAN KNOW

God hears your prayers and answers them. God loves for you to talk to Him.

I CAN LEARN

Draw a line from A to J. Write or draw something on the hands that you want to talk to Jesus about.

I CAN PRAY

WEEK #13

Tell God what you wrote or drew in the picture.

I CAN KNOW

As Jesus opens the scroll, four horses and their riders are used to describe what is going to happen on earth.

I CAN LEARN

Use the color key to color the horses.

1 = White
2 = Red
3 = Black
4 = Yellow

WAY TO GO!

I CAN PRAY

Tell God thank you for being in control of everything.

WEEK #13

103

SUNDAY

I CAN KNOW

The Bible says God will punish those who do not believe in His Son, Jesus.

I CAN LEARN

There will be terrible things happening, but if you trust Jesus as Savior from your sin, you will be in heaven when these things happen. Answer the questions.

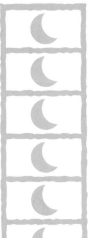

6 5 4 3 2 1   6 5 4 3 2 1

How many ☀s?	3	6	2	4
How many 🌙s?	7	4	3	5
How many ⭐s?	6	3	5	7

I CAN PRAY

Pray for your friends that don't know Jesus as their Savior.

WEEK #14

THE BIBLE SAYS

Revelation 7:2-3

MONDAY

I CAN KNOW

God promises to protect His children by putting a seal on them.

I CAN LEARN

Draw a ———— under the set that has more.

I CAN PRAY

Thank God for protecting you.

WEEK #14

105

TUESDAY

THE BIBLE SAYS
Revelation 7:16-17

I CAN KNOW
In heaven there will be no more hunger, thirst, pain or tears. Jesus will be like a shepherd and lead His children to springs of living water.

I CAN LEARN

Draw a ———— from Jesus to the springs of living water.

I CAN PRAY
Tell God thank you for making heaven such a wonderful place.

WEEK #14

WEDNESDAY

I CAN KNOW

Angels are God's special messengers. You can be a messenger for God, too, by telling others about Jesus.

I CAN LEARN

Write each missing number.

1 2 __ 4

5 6 __ 8

3 4 5 __

7 __ 9 10

I CAN PRAY

Ask God to help you be a special messenger for Him.

WEEK #14

107

I CAN KNOW

God is in control of everything; He even controls the animals. God will tell the locusts what to do.

I CAN LEARN

Color what God told the locusts not to harm.

I CAN PRAY

Tell God thank you for being in control.

WEEK #14

108

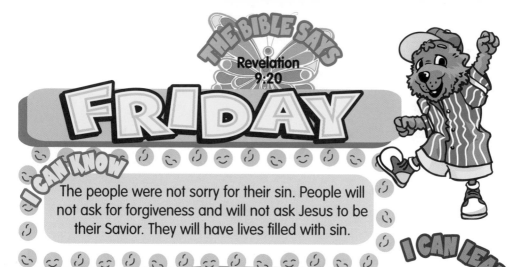

FRIDAY

I CAN KNOW

The people were not sorry for their sin. People will not ask for forgiveness and will not ask Jesus to be their Savior. They will have lives filled with sin.

I CAN LEARN

Circle the words that the idols are made of that people worship.

```
X  S  X  X  X  W  O  O  D  X
X  I  X  X  X  X  X  X  X  X
X  L  X  X  S  X  X  X  D  X
X  V  X  S  X  T  X  L  X  X
X  E  A  X  X  X  O  X  X  X
X  R  X  X  X  G  X  N  X  X
B  X  X  X  X  X  X  X  E  X
```

BRASS   GOLD   SILVER
STONE   WOOD

I CAN PRAY

Ask God to help you obey and do things that please Him.

WEEK #14

109

I CAN KNOW

God's Word is sweet to the hearts of those who love Jesus, but it is sour to those who do not love Jesus.

I CAN LEARN

You need to tell others about Jesus. Draw a ◯ around the pictures that show where you can tell others about Jesus.

WAY TO GO!

I CAN PRAY

Ask God to help you obey and be kind to others.

WEEK #14

110

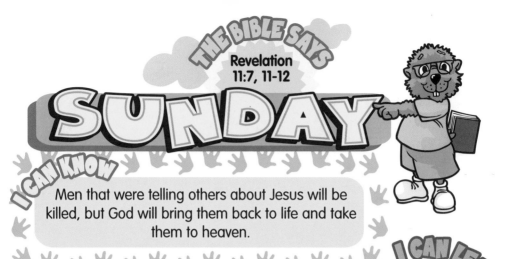

Revelation 11:7, 11-12

SUNDAY

I CAN KNOW

Men that were telling others about Jesus will be killed, but God will bring them back to life and take them to heaven.

I CAN LEARN

Draw a ——— to lead the two men to heaven.

Heaven

I CAN PRAY

Ask God to help you tell others about Jesus.

WEEK #15

111

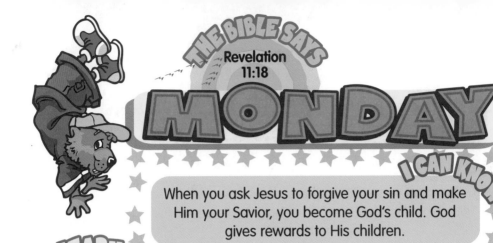

I CAN KNOW

When you ask Jesus to forgive your sin and make Him your Savior, you become God's child. God gives rewards to His children.

I CAN LEARN

Hold your book in front of a mirror to read the word.

REWARD

I CAN PRAY

Tell God thank you for making you His child.

WEEK #15

I CAN KNOW

The devil is a liar and he wants you to do wrong.
God is truth and wants you to do right.

I CAN LEARN

Read the words on the left side and draw lines to match them to the correct pictures.

Right

Wrong

I CAN PRAY

WEEK #15

Ask God to help you do the right things today.

THE BIBLE SAYS
Revelation 12:12

WEDNESDAY

The devil only has a little time left on earth. He will try harder to lie to people. God is so much greater than the devil, so the devil can never win.

I CAN LEARN

The words Great and God begin with the letter sound G. Draw a ☐ around the pictures that begin with the letter sound G. Trace the word God on the line.

I CAN PRAY

WEEK #15

Tell God thank you for being so great.

I CAN KNOW

Anyone who has not asked Jesus to be his Savior will be worshipping the devil. The book of life belongs to Jesus, and He will have everyone's name in it that accepts Him as their Savior from sin.

I CAN LEARN

Draw a line from 1 to 12. If you have accepted Jesus as your Savior, write your name in the book. If you have never accepted Jesus as your Savior and want to now, bow your head and pray and tell Him.

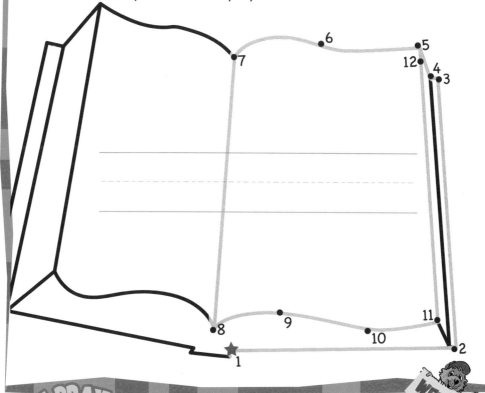

I CAN PRAY

Pray for your friends and family who don't have Jesus as their Savior.

WEEK #15

FRIDAY

I CAN KNOW

People on earth will think that the beast is good, but he is not.

I CAN LEARN

When you know God's Word, the Bible, the devil can't trick you into believing him. Draw a ◯ around the picture that shows how you can know God's Word.

I CAN PRAY

Ask God to help you be a good listener of His Word.

WEEK #15

116

SATURDAY

I CAN KNOW

The Good News of Jesus is for everyone. No matter your age, what language you speak or where you are from, Jesus wants you to know Him as your Savior.

I CAN LEARN

Draw a ⭕ around the pictures of people who the Good News is for.

WAY TO GO!

I CAN PRAY

Tell God thank you for loving everyone.

WEEK #15

117

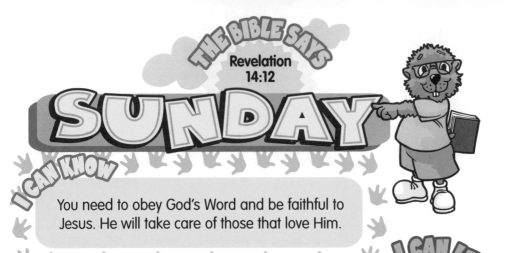

I CAN KNOW

You need to obey God's Word and be faithful to Jesus. He will take care of those that love Him.

I CAN LEARN

Help these children make the right choice for Jesus. Draw a line from the child to the choice they need to make.

I CAN PRAY

Ask Jesus to help you make the right choices.

WEEK #16

118

Revelation
14:14

MONDAY

I CAN KNOW

John saw Jesus sitting on a cloud. He was looking for everyone who had been faithful or unfaithful to Him.

I CAN LEARN

You can not hide from Jesus. ◯ the ♥ hidden in the picture. Trace on the line who you cannot hide from.

Jesus

I CAN PRAY

WEEK #16

Ask Jesus to help you be faithful to Him.

119

THE BIBLE SAYS
Revelation 15:3-4
TUESDAY

The faithful people will sing to God. They will sing about His great and marvelous works.

I CAN LEARN

You can sing to God, too. Make up a song about how great God is, and sing it to someone today. Draw a ☐ around the musical note that does not belong in each row.

I CAN PRAY

Tell God thank you for being so great and marvelous.

WEEK #16

WEDNESDAY

I CAN KNOW

After all the punishments of God, people will still not accept Jesus as Savior from their sin. The people will suffer by these judgments. But they will refuse to do what is right.

I CAN LEARN

Color the picture that shows how you should act toward God and your parents. Draw an X on the one that shows how you should not be.

I CAN PRAY

Ask God to show you when you need to ask for His forgiveness.

WEEK #16

THE BIBLE SAYS

Revelation 16:15-16

THURSDAY

Jesus wants you to be ready when He comes back to earth to take all Christians to heaven with Him. Be watchful. Be ready.

You can be ready for Jesus by obeying the Bible. Draw a line from 2 to 20. Count by twos.

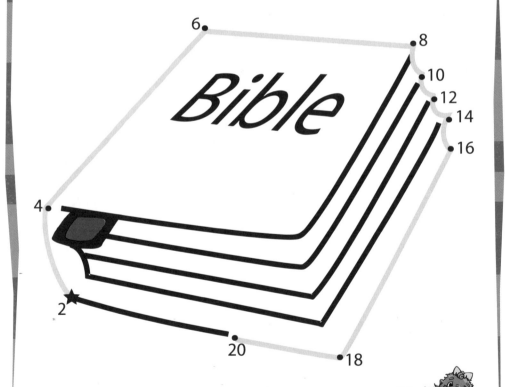

WEEK #16

Ask God to help you obey His Word, the Bible.

FRIDAY

Have you asked Jesus to be your Savior? Is your name written in the book of life?

If you have asked Jesus to be your Savior, write your name in the book. If you need help asking Jesus to be your Savior, talk to an adult. If you know someone who needs Jesus, write his name on the other page and pray for him now.

WEEK #16

Tell Jesus thank you for coming to be the Savior for everyone, including you.

123

I CAN KNOW

God has a plan. Everything that will happen is part of that plan.

I CAN LEARN

You can trust God that His plan is the best. Draw a line to take the children to whom they should trust for the best plan. Trace the word.

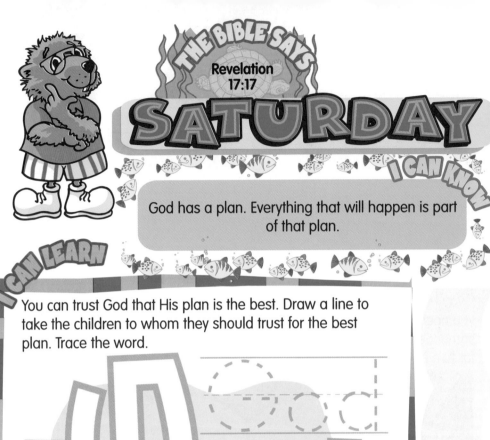

WAY TO GO!

I CAN PRAY

Ask God to show you what you need to do for Him today.

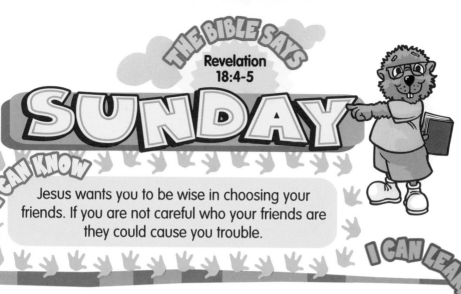

SUNDAY

THE BIBLE SAYS
Revelation 18:4-5

I CAN KNOW

Jesus wants you to be wise in choosing your friends. If you are not careful who your friends are they could cause you trouble.

I CAN LEARN

Color the picture of the friends that are doing right. Draw an **X** over the ones that are doing wrong.

I CAN PRAY

Ask Jesus to help you choose good friends.

WEEK #17

God is going to destroy the great city of Babylon in one hour because the people keep sinning.

I CAN LEARN

When you sin, you need to ask God to forgive you. Color the city of Babylon using the color key.

1 = blue

2 = red

3 = green

4 = yellow

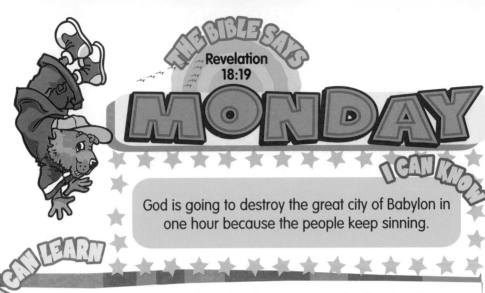

I CAN PRAY

Tell God how much you love Him for forgiving you from your sin.

WEEK #17

TUESDAY

I CAN KNOW

After Babylon is destroyed, there will not be anything or anyone left in the city. No musicians, craftsmen or even a light will be left. God hates sin, and He will punish it.

I CAN LEARN

Draw a ⭕ around the things that God will destroy in Babylon.

I CAN PRAY

Ask God to help you say no to sin.

WEEK #17

127

WEDNESDAY

THE BIBLE SAYS
Revelation 19:6

I CAN KNOW

There will be many people praising God. A loud choir will be singing "Hallelujah!" because God is the King over all the earth.

I CAN LEARN

Hold your book in front of a mirror. What word do you see? Tell God "Hallelujah!" for being the King over all the earth.

HALLELUJAH

I CAN PRAY

Praise God for all He has done for you.

WEEK #17

128

God has invited you to a great wedding.

I CAN LEARN

The wedding feast is for those who have been faithful and have asked Jesus to be their Savior. It will be a great feast. There will be great food there. Pick one food from each group and draw it on the plate.

I CAN PRAY

Praise Jesus for loving you so much.

WEEK #17

129

FRIDAY

In the end Jesus has all the victory over Satan's followers. Satan is a liar, but you can know that Jesus always speaks truth.

I CAN LEARN

Draw a —— to match the opposites.

Truth

full

down

off

empty

Liar

on

up

I CAN PRAY

WEEK #17

Tell Jesus thank you for always speaking the truth.

130

I CAN KNOW

The end has come for the devil. He will be locked away in a bottomless pit for 1,000 years. Jesus has the victory over sin and Satan. You can have victory over sin by obeying the Bible.

I CAN LEARN

Victory begins with the letter sound v. Draw a ◯ around the pictures that begin with the letter sound v. Write the letter V on the line.

WAY TO GO!

I CAN PRAY

Tell Jesus thank you for giving you victory over your sin.

WEEK #17

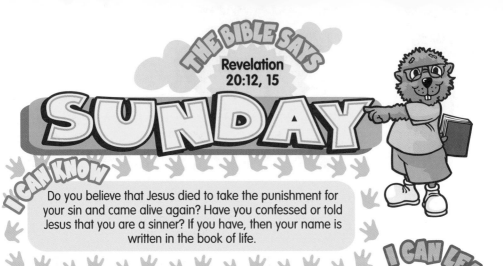

Do you believe that Jesus died to take the punishment for your sin and came alive again? Have you confessed or told Jesus that you are a sinner? If you have, then your name is written in the book of life.

I CAN LEARN

Color the next book.

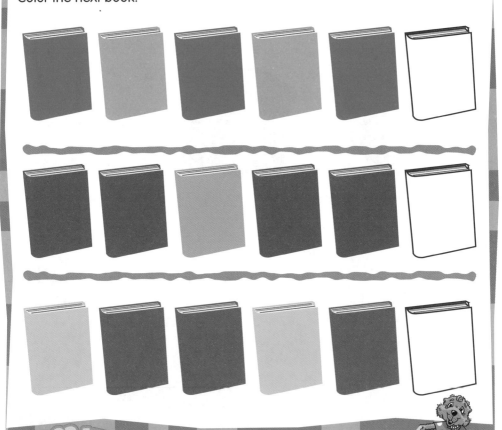

Tell Jesus thank you for taking the punishment for your sin.

WEEK #18

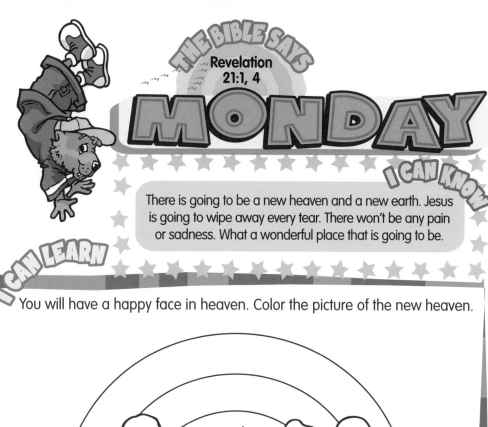

I CAN KNOW

There is going to be a new heaven and a new earth. Jesus is going to wipe away every tear. There won't be any pain or sadness. What a wonderful place that is going to be.

I CAN LEARN

You will have a happy face in heaven. Color the picture of the new heaven.

I CAN PRAY

Thank God for making heaven such a wonderful place.

WEEK #18

133

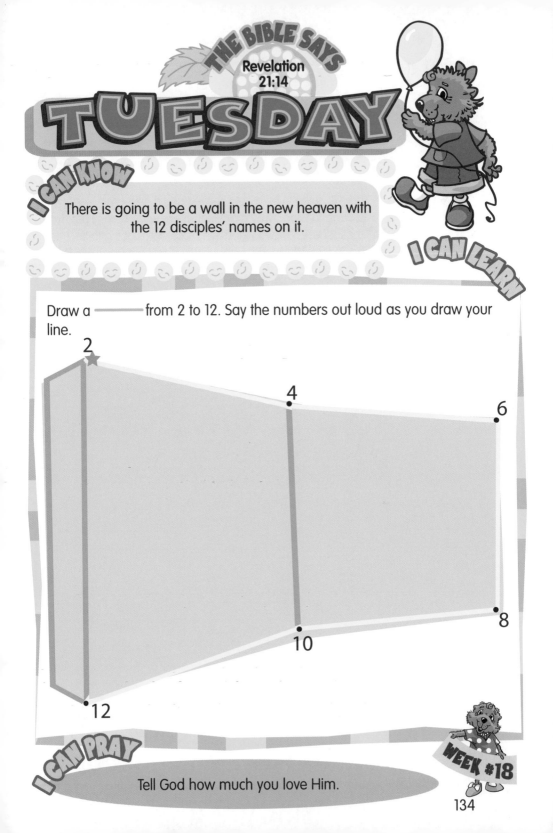

THE BIBLE SAYS

Revelation 21:14

TUESDAY

I CAN KNOW

There is going to be a wall in the new heaven with the 12 disciples' names on it.

I CAN LEARN

Draw a ——— from 2 to 12. Say the numbers out loud as you draw your line.

2

4

6

10

8

12

I CAN PRAY

Tell God how much you love Him.

WEEK #18

THE BIBLE SAYS

Revelation 21:23

WEDNESDAY

I CAN KNOW

There will be no need of a sun or moon in the new city of Jerusalem because God will be like a light.

I CAN LEARN

There will not be any darkness; God will take care of the light. Color the circles **yellow**.

I CAN PRAY

Tell God thank you for taking care of you.

WEEK #18

135

You will be able to serve God in heaven. You can serve Him now while you live here on earth.

I CAN LEARN

Draw a ◯ around the child that is serving God.

I CAN PRAY

Thank God for His beauty and brightness.

WEEK #18

FRIDAY

I CAN KNOW

God will reward you if you are faithful to Him.

I CAN LEARN

You can be faithful to God by obeying Him. Obey begins with the letter sound O. Trace the word obey.

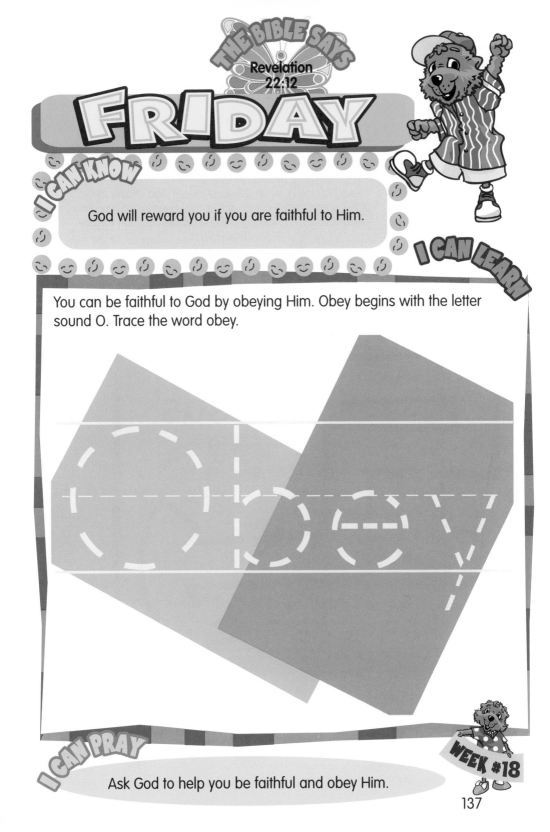

I CAN PRAY

Ask God to help you be faithful and obey Him.

WEEK #18

137

I CAN KNOW

Jesus is coming again. Nobody except God knows when He will come back to earth again. You need to tell everyone about Jesus and how He is the only one who can forgive from sin.

I CAN LEARN

Write down the name of a friend or family member on the line at the start of the maze that you want to tell about Jesus.

Jesus

WAY TO GO!

I CAN PRAY

Pray for the person whose name you wrote on the line.

WEEK #18

138

SUNDAY

God helped King David when he was in trouble. David kept his promise to Bathsheba. He chose their son, Solomon, to be the next king.

Find the three hidden letters in the palace and trace them on the line.

will help you when you are in trouble.

WEEK #19

Ask God to help you when you are having troubles.

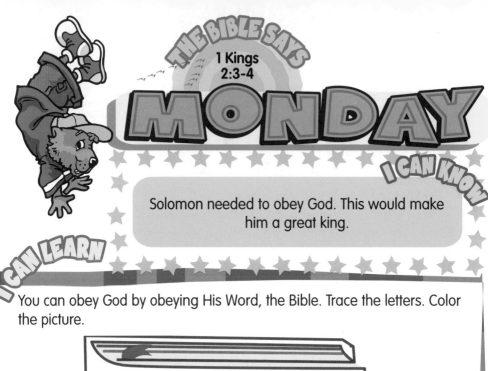

I CAN KNOW

Solomon needed to obey God. This would make him a great king.

I CAN LEARN

You can obey God by obeying His Word, the Bible. Trace the letters. Color the picture.

Holy Bible

I CAN PRAY

Tell God thank you for His Word, the Bible, written to you.

WEEK #19

I CAN KNOW

King Solomon asked God to make him a good king. He wanted to please God.

I CAN LEARN

You will please God if you are good and kind. Draw a ⭕ around the children that are pleasing God.

I CAN PRAY

WEEK #19

Ask God to help you be good and kind.

141

I CAN KNOW

All the people in Israel honored King Solomon. They knew God was helping him to make right choices.

I CAN LEARN

God will help you make right choices, too. Trace the letters in the puzzle.

Across
King _ _ _ _ _ _ _ made right choices.

Down
_ _ _ helped King Solomon make right choices.

I CAN PRAY

Ask God to help you make right choices.

WEEK #19

142

God gave King Solomon his wisdom and power. He was the wisest man in the world.

People came from far away to meet with King Solomon. Draw a ▬▬▬ to lead the people to King Solomon.

I CAN PRAY

Ask God to help you listen to wise people.

FRIDAY

I CAN KNOW

King Solomon built the temple as a special place for people to worship God. God's people first worshipped in a large tent, then the temple and now the church.

I CAN LEARN

Draw a ▢ around the picture where you go to worship God.

I CAN PRAY

WEEK #19

Tell God thank you for your church.

I CAN KNOW

King Solomon turned away from God. Even though he was wise, he made the wrong choice.

I CAN LEARN

You need to make right choices for God. Color the picture of the child making the right choice. Draw an X on the child making the wrong choice.

WAY TO GO!

I CAN PRAY

Ask God to forgive you for something you have done wrong.

WEEK #19

145

THE BIBLE SAYS

1 Kings 12:8

SUNDAY

I CAN KNOW

The new king, Rehoboam, listened to his friends. He should have listened to the older and wiser men. He made a bad choice.

I CAN LEARN

You need to listen to wise people. Draw a ——— to the people King Rehoboam listened to. Draw a ——— to the people you should listen to.

I CAN PRAY

Ask God to help you listen to your parents.

WEEK #20

146

I CAN KNOW

God didn't want Rehoboam to fight against his own people. You should get along with your brothers, sisters and friends. God wants you to be kind to others.

I CAN LEARN

Kind begins with the letter sound K. Draw a △ around the pictures that start with the letter sound K. Write the letter K on the line.

I CAN PRAY

Ask God to help you be kind to others.

WEEK #20

147

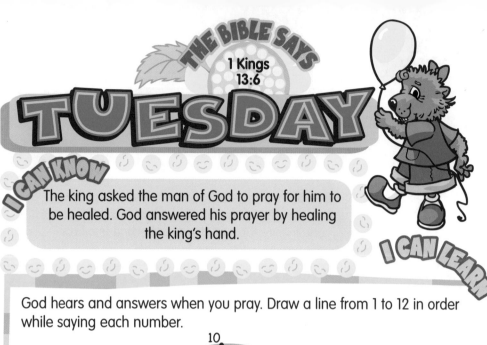

THE BIBLE SAYS
1 Kings 13:6
TUESDAY

I CAN KNOW

The king asked the man of God to pray for him to be healed. God answered his prayer by healing the king's hand.

I CAN LEARN

God hears and answers when you pray. Draw a line from 1 to 12 in order while saying each number.

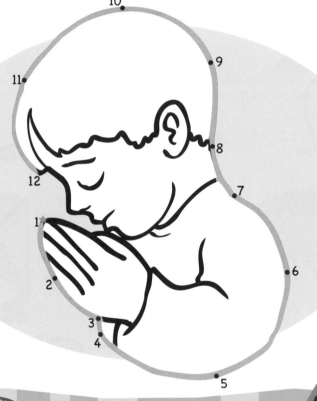

I CAN PRAY

Pray for someone who is sick.

WEDNESDAY

I CAN KNOW

The man of God was supposed to go straight home. Another man lied to him and tricked him into disobeying God. God said he would be punished for disobeying Him and listening to lies.

I CAN LEARN

God wants you to obey Him and not tell lies. Draw an **X** over the word that God does not want you to do. ◯ what God wants you to do.

Lie

Obey

I CAN PRAY

Ask God to help you tell the truth.

WEEK #20

149

God gave Elijah the food and water he needed. God used birds and a small brook to take care of Elijah.

I CAN LEARN

God takes care of you, too. Use the key to color the picture of Elijah by the brook.

Black =   Blue =

Green =   Red =

I CAN PRAY

WEEK #20

Tell God thank you for the food He gives you.

FRIDAY

I CAN KNOW

The woman helped Elijah by making him food. God gave the widow and her son all the food she needed because she helped Elijah.

I CAN LEARN

You can help others, too. Draw a ○ around the pictures you could use to make somebody a snack or a meal. Count the pictures you circled and write the number in the space.

I CAN PRAY

Pray for an older person who needs help.

WEEK #20

I CAN KNOW

God was going to send rain. He is the only One who controls the weather.

I CAN LEARN

Draw a △ around the raindrops that are the same.

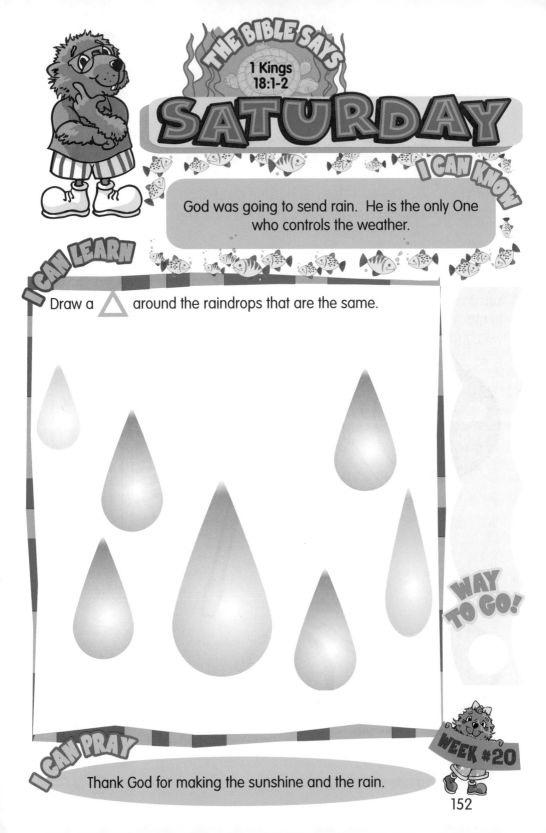

WAY TO GO!

WEEK #20

I CAN PRAY

Thank God for making the sunshine and the rain.

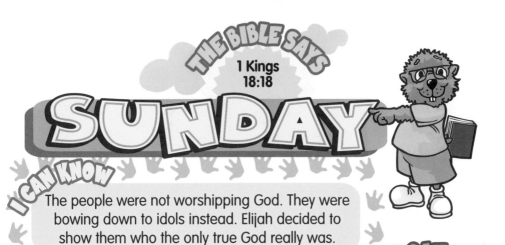

I CAN KNOW

The people were not worshipping God. They were bowing down to idols instead. Elijah decided to show them who the only true God really was.

I CAN LEARN

There is only one God. You should worship Him. ⭕ all the number 1's hidden in the picture. Write the number 1 on the line.

I CAN PRAY

Praise God for being the one true God.

WEEK # 21

153

I CAN KNOW

God sent fire from heaven to show all the people that He was the only God.

I CAN LEARN

Fire begins with the letter sound F. Trace the letter F on the line. Draw a line from the letter F to the pictures whose beginning sound starts with F.

I CAN PRAY

Tell God thank you for His great power.

WEEK #21

154

THE BIBLE SAYS
1 Kings 18:46

TUESDAY

I CAN KNOW

Elijah told King Ahab to go home because it was going to rain. Ahab got into his chariot and hurried home. Elijah ran in the power of the Lord and got to Jezreel before Ahab.

I CAN LEARN

God is very powerful. Draw 2 lines to take King Ahab and Elijah back to Jezreel.

I CAN PRAY

Ask God for something you or your family needs.

WEEK #21

WEDNESDAY

I CAN KNOW

God spoke to Elijah in a quiet whisper and asked him why he was running away. Elijah listened to the quiet voice of God.

I CAN LEARN

You need to listen to God. Draw a ☐ around the ways you can listen to God.

I CAN PRAY

Thank God for the Bible.

WEEK #21

I CAN KNOW

Naboth wouldn't sell King Ahab his vineyard. The king pouted because he didn't get what he wanted.

I CAN LEARN

When you do not get your way, you should not pout and become angry. God wants you to be happy with what you have. Draw a line to the picture to finish the sentence.

When I do not get what I want I...

I CAN PRAY

Ask God to help you be thankful.

WEEK #21

THE BIBLE SAYS

1 Kings 21:25-29

FRIDAY

I CAN KNOW

Ahab was a wicked king. God said He had to punish him. Ahab was sorry for his sin.

I CAN LEARN

Put the first letter of each picture in the box to see what God will do when you ask.

_ _ _ _ _ _ _

_ _ _ _ _ _ _ _ _ _ _ _ _

_ _ _ _ _ _ _

I CAN PRAY

Ask God to forgive you for something you have done wrong.

WEEK #21

158

King Ahab tried to trick the other army. He knew they were after him. Even then, God was in control.

I CAN LEARN

God is in control all the time. Circle the times that God is in control.

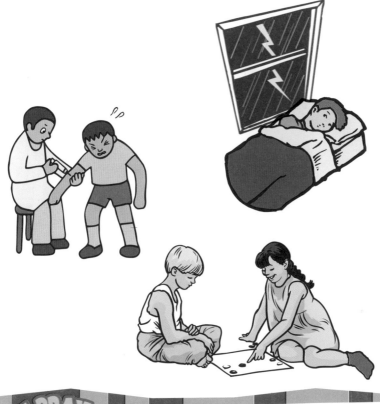

WAY TO GO!

I CAN PRAY

Thank Jesus for dying on the cross for you.

I CAN KNOW

King Ahaziah did not get well because he did not ask God. He wanted to ask false gods if he would be healed.

I CAN LEARN

God wants to hear your prayers when you need help. He is the one true God. Draw a circle around each picture that has only one object. Trace the word one.

God

one

I CAN PRAY

Thank God for being the one true God and listening to your prayers.

WEEK #22

160

I CAN KNOW

God took Elijah to heaven in a chariot of fire, and he did not burn or die. One day you will go to heaven if you believe Jesus died for your sin and ask Him to forgive you.

I CAN LEARN

Draw a line to take Elijah to heaven.

Heaven

I CAN PRAY

Tell God thank you for making a way for you to go to heaven.

WEEK #22

THE BIBLE SAYS

2 Kings 2:14-15

TUESDAY

Elisha took Elijah's place as a prophet for Israel. All the people knew it because he took Elijah's coat after Elijah went to heaven. A prophet was a man who would speak for God to the people.

I CAN LEARN

Draw a ——— from 1 to 10 to complete the picture.

I CAN PRAY

WEEK #22

Pray for the pastor at your church.

162

WEDNESDAY

THE BIBLE SAYS

2 Kings 4:9-10

I CAN KNOW

The Shunammite woman helped take care of Elisha. She built a special room just for him.

I CAN LEARN

You can take care of guests in your home, too. What did the Shunammite woman put in Elisha's room? Draw a line from the pictures to the room.

I CAN PRAY

Ask God to help you be kind to guests in your home.

WEEK #22

163

Elisha prayed for the dead boy. God made the boy come alive again.

I CAN LEARN

God hears you when you pray to Him. Write a 1 by what happed first. Write a 2 by what happened next. Write a 3 by what happened last.

I CAN PRAY

WEEK #22

Tell God thank you for hearing you when you pray.

THE BIBLE SAYS

2 Kings 4:42-43

FRIDAY

I CAN KNOW

There was not enough food for the people. A man brought 20 loaves of bread to help feed the people. He did not think it would be enough, but Elisha knew there would be leftovers. He trusted God to provide more than enough food.

I CAN LEARN

You can trust God to provide food for you. Draw a ———— to the coin that you will need to buy each food.

10¢

25¢

1¢

I CAN PRAY

Tell God thank you for the good food He gives you to eat.

WEEK #22

165

Naaman was healed when he obeyed God. Sometimes God's instructions may seem strange to you, but you still need to obey.

I CAN LEARN

Write the missing numbers.

1

5

WAY TO GO!

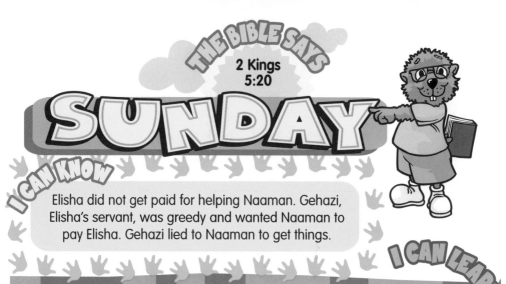

I CAN KNOW

Elisha did not get paid for helping Naaman. Gehazi, Elisha's servant, was greedy and wanted Naaman to pay Elisha. Gehazi lied to Naaman to get things.

I CAN LEARN

When you tell a lie you are disobeying God. You should always tell the truth. Truth begins with the letter sound Tr. Draw a △ around the pictures that begin with the letter sound Tr. Trace the word Truth.

I CAN PRAY

Ask God to always help you tell the truth.

WEEK #23

167

THE BIBLE SAYS

2 Kings 6:5-7

MONDAY

One of the men lost a borrowed axe in the water and was upset. God helped Elisha perform a miracle. Things made of metal like an axe can not float.

Only God can make metal float. Find 5 hidden axes in the picture and ◯ them.

Thank God for watching over you.

WEEK #23

THE BIBLE SAYS

2 Kings 6:22

TUESDAY

I CAN KNOW

Elisha told the king of Israel to be kind to those that were unkind. He was to give them food and water instead of hurting them.

I CAN LEARN

You need to be kind to others even when they are treating you badly. Color the picture. Tell your mom or dad what you would do if this were you.

I CAN PRAY

Ask God to help you be kind to those who treat you unkindly.

WEEK #23

169

I CAN KNOW

The king felt sorry for the woman that talked to him. You should feel sorry for people who are sad.

I CAN LEARN

Draw a circle around the pictures that show how you can help somebody who is sad.

I CAN PRAY

WEEK #23

Ask God to help you know what to say to others when they are sad.

The Syrians left their camp because they were scared. God made loud noises to make them think they were being attacked. Now God's people were safe.

I CAN LEARN

God will keep you safe, too. Circle the number.

1   2   3

1   2   3

1   2   3

1   2   3

I CAN PRAY

Ask God to keep you safe today.

WEEK #23

FRIDAY

I CAN KNOW

Elisha told the people what was going to happen the next day. There was food in the land to sell, and it sold for the price he said. Elisha had spoken the truth.

I CAN LEARN

God had told Elisha what to speak. God speaks to you through His Word, the Bible. Circle what you use to speak with.

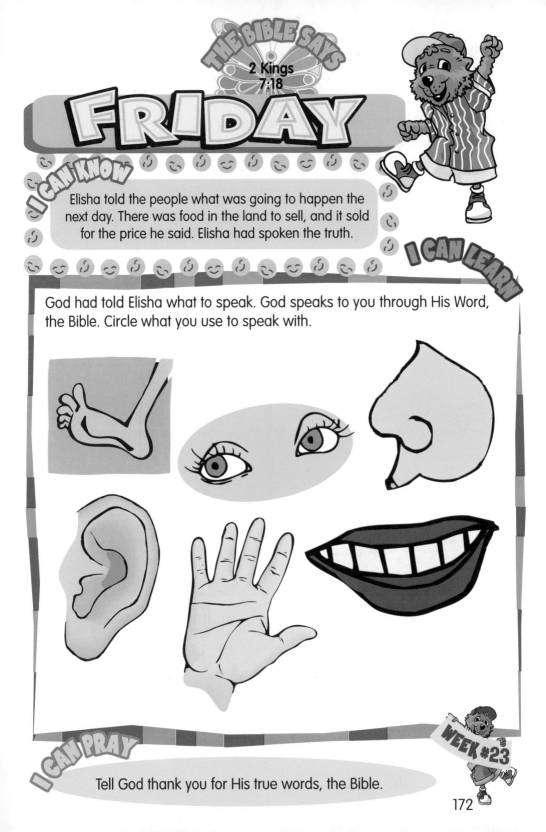

I CAN PRAY

Tell God thank you for His true words, the Bible.

WEEK #23

172

I CAN KNOW

Elisha sent a man to tell Jehu that he will be the next king over Israel. He was to hurry and pour oil on Jehu's head so the people would know that he was the new king.

I CAN LEARN

God picks people for different jobs. Draw a line to take the man quickly to Jehu to make him king.

WAY TO GO!

I CAN PRAY

Tell God thank you that He makes plans for you and knows everything you will do.

WEEK #23

173

SUNDAY

A man died and his friends threw him in Elisha's grave. When he touched Elisha's bones, he came back to life.

I CAN LEARN

Only God could do this miracle. Write a 1 by what happened first. Write a 2 by what happened next.

I CAN PRAY

WEEK #24

Pray for someone you know who is sick.

174

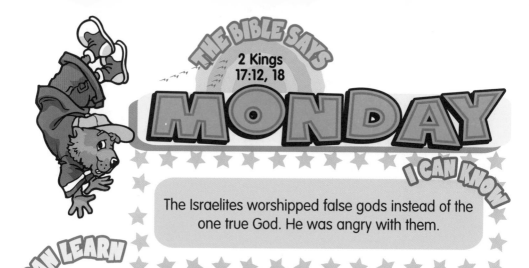

I CAN KNOW

The Israelites worshipped false gods instead of the one true God. He was angry with them.

I CAN LEARN

Draw a circle around the one thing you should worship.

God

I CAN PRAY

WEEK #24

Ask God to help you only worship Him.

175

TUESDAY

I CAN KNOW

God will take care of your enemies. You don't have to fight or say bad things to them.

I CAN LEARN

Find the hidden word God in the picture.

God

I CAN PRAY

Tell God thank you for taking care of your enemies.

WEEK #24

176

WEDNESDAY

I CAN KNOW

The idols that the people were worshipping could burn. But God is the one true God.

I CAN LEARN

God should be first place in your life. Use the color key to color the first place ribbon to remind you to always put God first.

1 = purple
2 = yellow

I CAN PRAY

Ask God to help you put Him first place in your life.

WEEK #24

177

Hezekiah was very sick. He prayed to God and asked him to look at his life. God heard his prayers and promised to heal him.

Hold your book in front of the mirror to see how Hezekiah lived. You need to live this way, too.

good

heart

WEEK #24

Ask God to give you a happy heart today.

FRIDAY

I CAN KNOW

Hezekiah was prideful of all his treasures and worldly goods. He was making them more important than God. He forgot that it was God who had given him all his treasures.

I CAN LEARN

Color the picture of Hezekiah's treasures. Trace the name of the person who gives you everything you have.

God

I CAN PRAY

WEEK #24

Ask God to help you not be proud today.

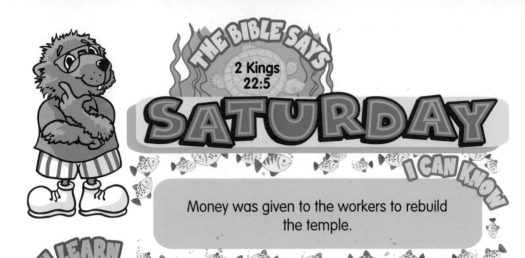

Money was given to the workers to rebuild the temple.

I CAN LEARN

Draw a line underneath what you can do to help your church look special for God.

WAY TO GO!

I CAN PRAY

Tell God thank you for the people who take care of your church.

WEEK #24

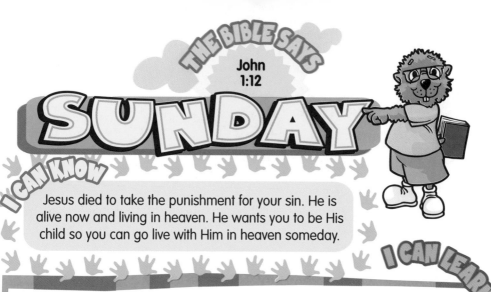

John 1:12

SUNDAY

I CAN KNOW

Jesus died to take the punishment for your sin. He is alive now and living in heaven. He wants you to be His child so you can go live with Him in heaven someday.

I CAN LEARN

You can be one of God's children if you accept Jesus as your Savior from sin. Draw a line from a to l to complete the picture.

I CAN PRAY

Tell Jesus thank you for taking the punishment for your sin.

WEEK #25

181

THE BIBLE SAYS

John 1:23

MONDAY

I CAN KNOW

God sent John to tell everyone that Jesus was coming soon.

I CAN LEARN

Draw a ——— from the store to the house. ◯ the places where you can tell others about Jesus.

FRESH VEGGIES

LIBRARY

I CAN PRAY

Tell God thank you for His Son, Jesus.

WEEK #25

182

THE BIBLE SAYS

John 1:29

TUESDAY

John saw Jesus walking toward him. He told everyone that Jesus was the Lamb of God. That means He is God's Son and He would take away their sin.

Jesus can take away your sin too. Lamb begins with the letter sound L. Draw a ——— from the lamb to the pictures that begin with the letter sound L.

Tell God thank you for His Son Jesus.

183

WEDNESDAY

THE BIBLE SAYS
John 1:45

I CAN KNOW

Philip was so excited that he had found Jesus. He went and told his friend Nathanael.

I CAN LEARN

You can tell your friends about Jesus too. Draw a △ around where you can take your friends to so they can learn about Jesus.

I CAN PRAY

WEEK #25

Ask Jesus to help you tell others about Him.

John 2:9, 11

THURSDAY

I CAN KNOW

Jesus turned water into wine at a wedding. This was His first miracle. Jesus' disciples believed in Him after they saw the miracle.

I CAN LEARN

You can believe in Jesus even without seeing a miracle. Draw a ☐ around the ways you can get to know Jesus.

I CAN PRAY

Ask Jesus to help you know Him better.

WEEK #25

FRIDAY

After Jesus came alive again, His friends finally believed all the words He had spoken.

Jesus speaks to you through His Word, the Bible. You need to listen when the Bible is read to you. Draw a ———— under the biggest one.

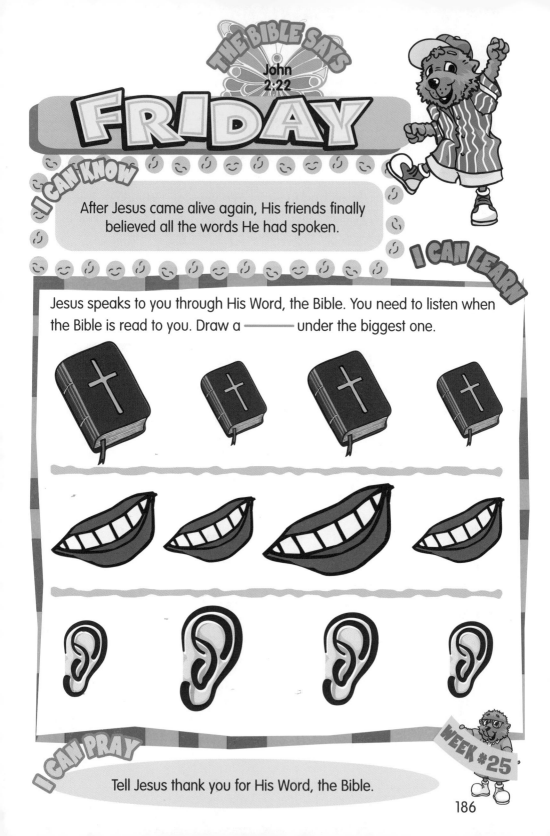

Tell Jesus thank you for His Word, the Bible.

I CAN KNOW

Jesus wants you to know that the most important thing is that you become one of His children. He loves you and wants you to be His child.

I CAN LEARN

If you have asked Jesus to be your Savior from sin then you are His child. Child begins with the letter sound ch.

○ the picture that begins with the letter sound ch.

WAY TO GO!

I CAN PRAY

Tell Jesus thank you for accepting you as His child.

WEEK #25

187

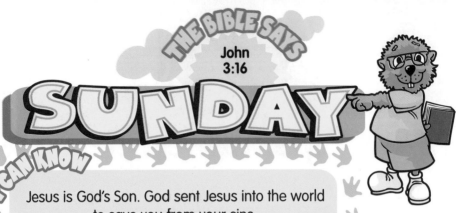

I CAN KNOW

Jesus is God's Son. God sent Jesus into the world to save you from your sins.

I CAN LEARN

Write or have someone write your name on the line. Color the heart.

God loves

_____

I CAN PRAY

Thank God for sending His Son, Jesus.

WEEK #26

188

When you believe in Jesus as your Savior from sin, you will live in heaven with God forever.

I CAN LEARN

You can live with God in heaven someday. Draw a line from the children to heaven.

Heaven

I CAN PRAY

WEEK #26

Pray for someone who doesn't believe in Jesus.

TUESDAY

I CAN KNOW

Your heart needs and wants Jesus. Once you ask Jesus to be your Savior, He never leaves.

I CAN LEARN

◯ the number that is the same as the word.

four	4	3	5	10
one	7	10	12	1
nine	5	9	6	8
two	1	12	2	4

I CAN PRAY

Thank God for always being with you.

WEEK #26

190

WEDNESDAY

I CAN KNOW

God wants you to be like the woman. He wants you to tell everyone about Jesus. Who can you tell today?

I CAN LEARN

You use your mouth to tell others about Jesus. Draw a ◯ around the 4 hidden lips, to remember to tell others about Jesus.

I CAN PRAY

Ask Jesus to help you tell others about Him.

WEEK #26

191

I CAN KNOW

After spending time with Jesus, many of the people believed that Jesus was the Savior of the world. You can spend time with Jesus by praying and reading your Bible.

I CAN LEARN

Color the pictures that show how you can spend time with Jesus.

I CAN PRAY

Ask Jesus to help you pray and read your Bible every day.

WEEK #26

192

FRIDAY

The man believed Jesus could make his son better. Jesus is God. He is powerful and can do wonderful things.

Jesus will keep His promises to you. What He says He will do. Write the number 1 beside what happened first. Write the number 2 beside what happened last.

Thank Jesus for something wonderful He has done in your life.

WEEK #26

When Jesus made someone better, it was called a miracle. It showed how great He was.

Only Jesus can do miracles. Color the picture.

1 = Brown
2 = Blue
3 = Green
4 = Yellow

WAY TO GO!

Pray for someone who is sick.

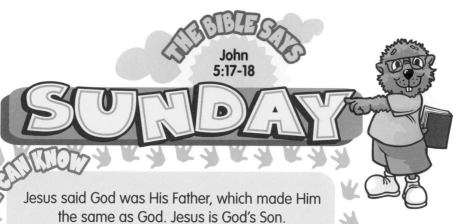

I CAN KNOW

Jesus said God was His Father, which made Him the same as God. Jesus is God's Son.

I CAN LEARN

Use a **Red** to trace the letters.

JESUS

IS

GOD

I CAN PRAY

WEEK #27

Pray for others to believe Jesus is God.

John 5:36

MONDAY

I CAN KNOW

I CAN LEARN

Jesus said and did many things to show the people that God sent Him. Jesus was doing what God wanted. He was obeying God.

You will be happy when you obey God. Draw a happy face below the pictures of children who are obeying God.

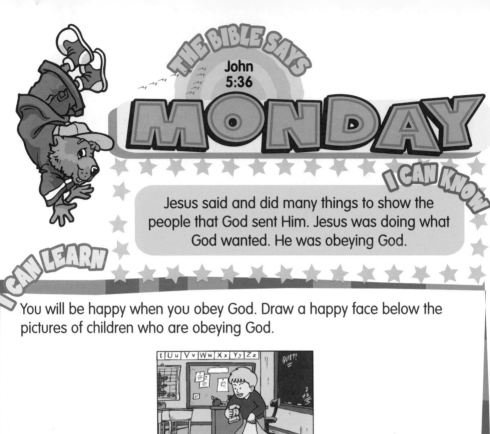

I CAN PRAY

WEEK #27

Ask God to help you obey Him.

196

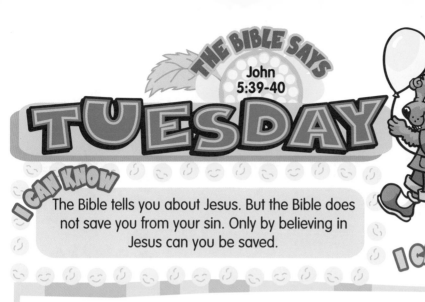

THE BIBLE SAYS

John 5:39-40

TUESDAY

The Bible tells you about Jesus. But the Bible does not save you from your sin. Only by believing in Jesus can you be saved.

Draw a line from 1 to 12 to complete the picture.

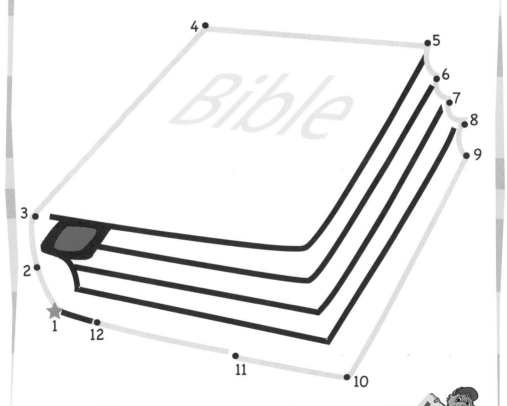

WEEK #27

Tell God thank you for giving you the Bible.

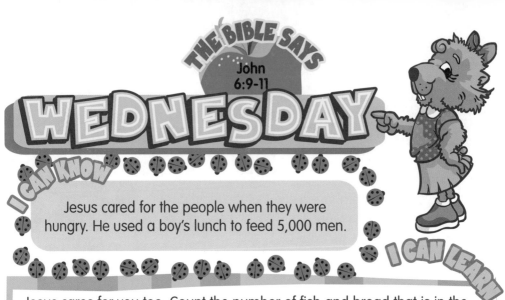

I CAN KNOW

Jesus cared for the people when they were hungry. He used a boy's lunch to feed 5,000 men.

I CAN LEARN

Jesus cares for you too. Count the number of fish and bread that is in the basket. Write your name on the line.

Jesus cares for _____.

I CAN PRAY

WEEK #27

Tell Jesus thank you for caring for you.

198

John
6:24

THURSDAY

I CAN KNOW

The crowd followed Jesus because He fed them. You should follow Jesus, too, because of what He has done for you.

I CAN LEARN

Draw a line to lead the people to Jesus.

I CAN PRAY

Ask Jesus to help you follow Him with a thankful heart.

WEEK #27

199

FRIDAY

Other people give us things or help us, but it all comes from God.

Match these helpers to the places they work.

Thank God for people who help you, like your parents and teachers.

WEEK #27

I CAN KNOW

God teaches you from the Bible. You should listen and learn all you can about Jesus.

I CAN LEARN

Draw a ☐ around the 6 hidden ears.

WAY TO GO!

I CAN PRAY

Ask God to help you listen and learn in Sunday school, church, and at home.

WEEK #27

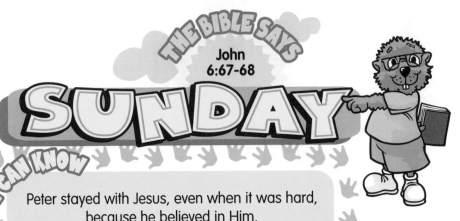

THE BIBLE SAYS

John 6:67-68

SUNDAY

I CAN KNOW

Peter stayed with Jesus, even when it was hard, because he believed in Him.

I CAN LEARN

It is not always easy to follow Jesus. Sometimes friends tease. Sometimes it is hard to obey the Bible. Help the girl follow Jesus by coloring in the rocks that have a cross on them.

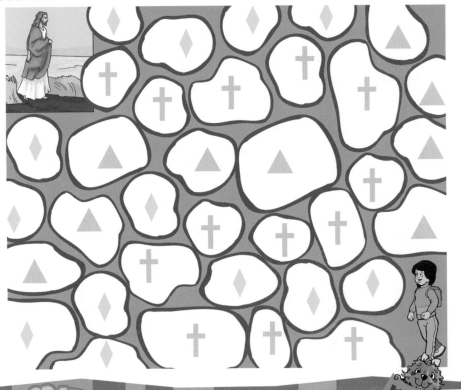

I CAN PRAY

WEEK #28

Ask Jesus to help you follow Him even when it is hard.

I CAN KNOW

Jesus told the people about the bad things they were doing. Some people liked the bad things, so they hated Jesus for telling them the truth.

I CAN LEARN

When you listen to and obey Jesus, you will be happy. Look at the picture and draw the missing parts.

I CAN PRAY

Ask Jesus to help you listen to and obey Him.

WEEK #28

I CAN KNOW

People were amazed at how much Jesus knew. He said His teaching was God's teaching. The Bible is God's teachings.

I CAN LEARN

You learn God's teaching from the Bible. Write the correct letter to finish the word.

I S B

Bible

I CAN PRAY

WEDNESDAY

I CAN KNOW

Jesus told the people that He knew God because He came from God.

I CAN LEARN

Draw a line from Jesus to earth. Jesus now lives in heaven with God. Do you want to be with Him in heaven someday?

I CAN PRAY

Thank Jesus for coming down to earth for you.

WEEK #28

I CAN KNOW

People began to believe Jesus was the Christ after listening to Him teach.

I CAN LEARN

Draw the missing body part that you use to hear with.

I CAN PRAY

Ask God to help you be a good listener of His Word, the Bible.

WEEK #28

206

FRIDAY

I CAN KNOW

Jesus knew that all people sin. You sin when you disobey God. When you tell God you are sorry for your sins, He forgives you.

I CAN LEARN

Draw an X on the pictures that are sin. Color the picture of the child asking God to forgive him.

I CAN PRAY

Ask God to help you forgive someone who has hurt you.

WEEK #28

I CAN KNOW

God loves you very much and wants you to live with Him someday. He doesn't want you to be separated from Him.

I CAN LEARN

You need to believe that Jesus took the punishment for your sin. Draw a line from 1 to 12. Color the picture.

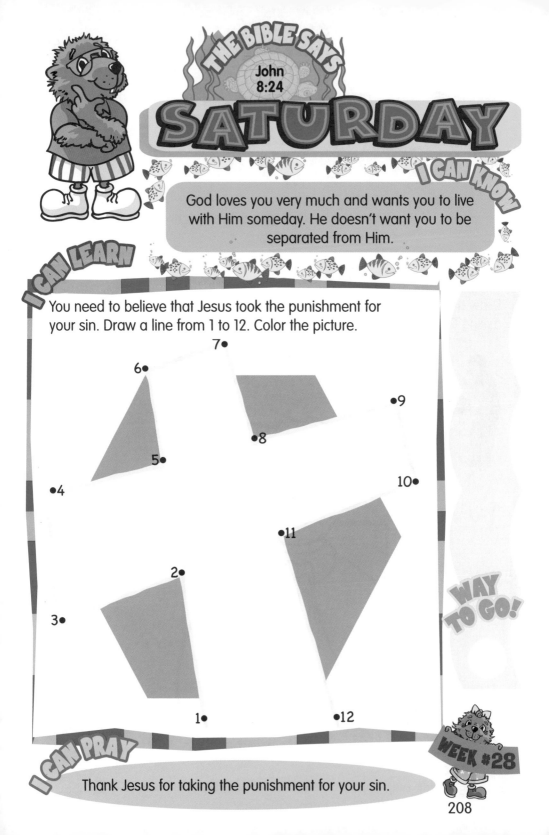

WAY TO GO!

I CAN PRAY

Thank Jesus for taking the punishment for your sin.

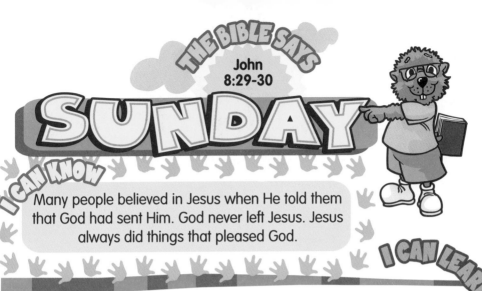

John
8:29-30

SUNDAY

I CAN KNOW

Many people believed in Jesus when He told them that God had sent Him. God never left Jesus. Jesus always did things that pleased God.

I CAN LEARN

Draw a ⭕ around 3 things that you can do that pleases God.

I CAN PRAY

Ask God to help you please Him everyday.

WEEK #29

209

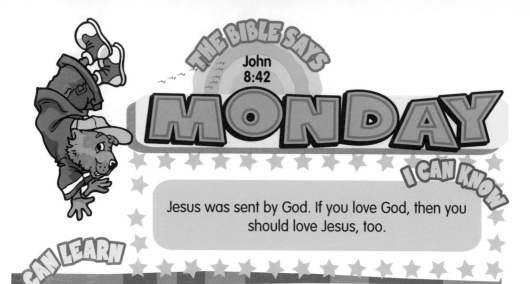

I CAN KNOW

Jesus was sent by God. If you love God, then you should love Jesus, too.

I CAN LEARN

Use a **red** crayon and trace the lines, then color in the letters to discover whom you should love.

I CAN PRAY

WEEK #29

Ask God to help you love Him with your whole heart.

I CAN KNOW

Jesus wants you to listen and obey what the Bible says.

I CAN LEARN

These children have listened to God's Word and are obeying God by obeying their parents and cleaning their room. Count the hidden crayons and write the number in the box and trace the word on the line.

SIX

I CAN PRAY

Ask God to help you listen and obey what the Bible says.

WEDNESDAY

I CAN KNOW

Jesus would heal the blind man to show how powerful and mighty God is.

I CAN LEARN

Write a number 1 by what happened first. Write 2 by what happened next. Write 3 by what happened last. Color in the missing parts to these pictures.

I CAN PRAY

Praise Jesus for being powerful and mighty.

WEEK #29

THE BIBLE SAYS

John 9:16

THURSDAY

I CAN KNOW

The people did not agree about who Jesus was. Some people said Jesus was a sinner because He worked on a holy day called the Sabbath. Other people said Jesus was good because He did miracles.

I CAN LEARN

Do you think Jesus was good or bad? Draw a happy face in the box if you think Jesus was good. Draw a sad face in the box if you think Jesus was bad.

I CAN PRAY

Ask Jesus to help you know and only believe the truth about Him.

WEEK #29

213

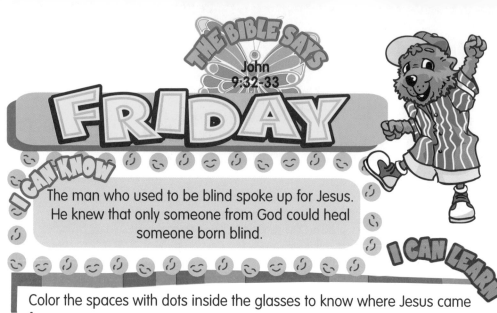

I CAN KNOW

The man who used to be blind spoke up for Jesus. He knew that only someone from God could heal someone born blind.

I CAN LEARN

Color the spaces with dots inside the glasses to know where Jesus came from.

from God

I CAN PRAY

Thank Jesus that He hears you when you pray.

WEEK #29

214

I CAN KNOW

The only way to be saved is through Jesus. He not only gives you life forever with Him, but He gives you a life full of joy on earth.

I CAN LEARN

Have you asked Jesus to save you from your sin. Help the children get to the person who can save them from their sin.

WAY TO GO!

I CAN PRAY

Tell Jesus thank you for giving you joy.

WEEK #29

215

John
10:27-28

SUNDAY

I CAN KNOW

If you are following Jesus, you are His forever. He is your Shepherd, and you are one of His sheep. There is no one or nothing that can take away your eternal life.

I CAN LEARN

Color the shepherd and count his sheep. Write the number inside the sheep as you count them.

I CAN PRAY

Thank Jesus for being the Good Shepherd who takes care of you.

WEEK #30

216

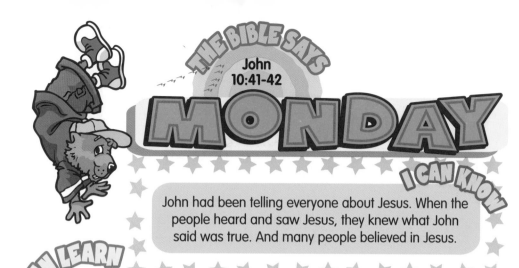

I CAN KNOW

John had been telling everyone about Jesus. When the people heard and saw Jesus, they knew what John said was true. And many people believed in Jesus.

I CAN LEARN

You should tell others what you know about Jesus, too. Circle the things that you can tell others about Jesus.

I CAN PRAY

Ask Jesus to help you tell others about Him.

WEEK #30

217

THE BIBLE SAYS

John 11:3

TUESDAY

Mary and Martha told Jesus that their brother, Lazarus, was sick. When you are sick or someone you know is sick, you can tell Jesus about it by praying to Him.

I CAN LEARN

Color these things that help when you are sick.

I CAN PRAY

WEEK #30

Pray for someone you know who is sick.

THE BIBLE SAYS
John 11:25

WEDNESDAY

The bad things you do, sin, keep you apart from God. Jesus died and came alive again to make a way for you to be close to God. Believing in Jesus is the way to be close to God.

I CAN LEARN

Draw a line from 1 to 12 to make a bridge so Jesus can lead the child to God and heaven.

Heaven

WEEK #30

Thank Jesus for making a way for you to be close to God.

John
11:43-44

THURSDAY

I CAN KNOW

Through God's power, Jesus did many miracles.
He even made people like Lazarus alive after they
had been dead. Jesus is all powerful.

I CAN LEARN

Write a 1 underneath what happened first. Write a 2 underneath what
happened next.

I CAN PRAY

Praise God for being so strong and mighty
and doing things for you.

WEEK #30

220

FRIDAY

THE BIBLE SAYS
John 11:45

I CAN KNOW

When people saw what Jesus had done, they believed in Him. They became children of God. The Bible tells us what Jesus has done.

I CAN LEARN

You can believe in Jesus as your Savior, too. All you need to do is ask Him to forgive your sin. If you believe in Jesus as your Savior, you can know Him better by reading your Bible. Draw a circle around the picture of the children who are learning about Jesus.

I CAN PRAY

Pray today that you and others will believe Jesus.

WEEK #30

221

Mary poured a jar of expensive perfume on Jesus' feet to show Him how much she loved Him.

I CAN LEARN

You can tell Jesus how much you love Him by singing a song to Him. Color the first jar red. Circle the third jar.

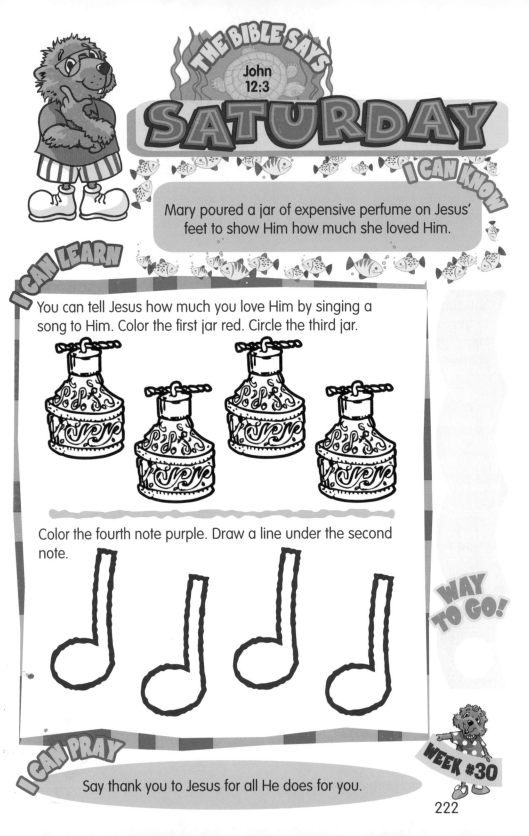

Color the fourth note purple. Draw a line under the second note.

WAY TO GO!

I CAN PRAY

Say thank you to Jesus for all He does for you.

WEEK #30

222

I CAN KNOW

The people were excited about Jesus. They praised Him by waving palm branches and shouting HOSANNA! You should be excited about Jesus and praise Him, too.

I CAN LEARN

Color this picture of the first Palm Sunday. Trace the word Hosanna.

Hosanna

I CAN PRAY

WEEK #31

Tell Jesus how great He is! Shout Hosanna!

John
12:26

MONDAY

If you want to please Jesus, you must do what the Bible says. When you obey God's Word, God is pleased with you and blesses you.

Draw a ☐ around the pictures of the children that are pleasing God.

Ask God to help you follow Him by obeying His Word.

I CAN KNOW

Your sin and all the sin in the world is like the dark. You cannot see which way to go. Jesus, who is perfect and does not sin, is the light in the darkness.

I CAN LEARN

Jesus helps you know what is right and do what is right. Use the key to color the picture.

○ = Yellow
△ = White
□ = Black

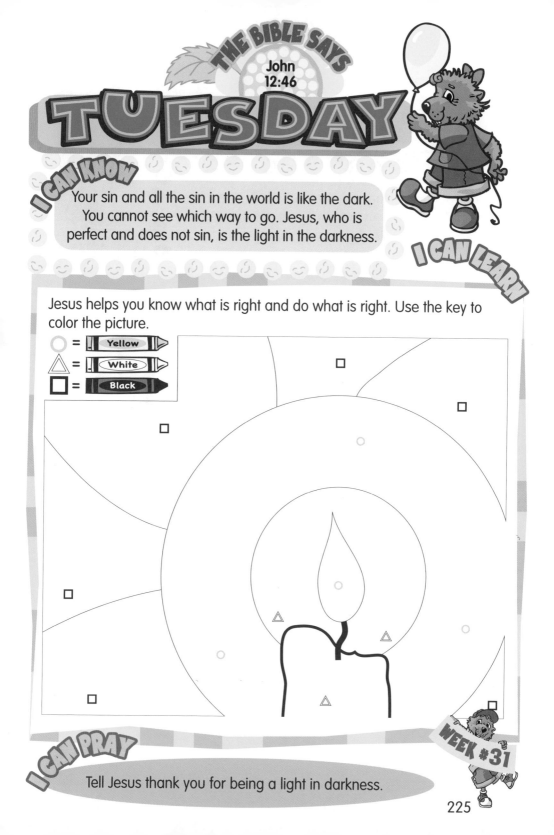

I CAN PRAY

Tell Jesus thank you for being a light in darkness.

WEEK #31

WEDNESDAY

THE BIBLE SAYS
John 13:5

I CAN KNOW

One way, Jesus showed His love was to wash His disciples' feet, even though it was not a very fun job. He was serving them.

I CAN LEARN

You need to serve others like Jesus did. Sometimes it may not be fun. Find the two hidden jars in the picture.

I CAN PRAY

WEEK #31

Ask Jesus to help you serve others even when you don't want to.

226

I CAN KNOW

Jesus did many great and wonderful things. He loved others. He helped and cared for others.

I CAN LEARN

You are to follow Jesus' example and love others by serving them. Draw a ◯ around the children who are showing love to others. Draw a ◯ around the way you want to serve someone today.

I CAN PRAY

Ask God to help you behave as Jesus did.

WEEK #31

227

FRIDAY

Jesus wants you to love others, because He loves you. Everyone will know that you love Jesus when you show your love to other people.

The people on the left are sad. Which picture on the right would show them Jesus' love and help them feel happy?

Ask Jesus to help you love other people as He loves you.

228

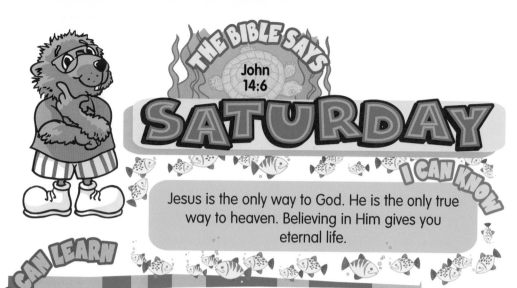

Jesus is the only way to God. He is the only true way to heaven. Believing in Him gives you eternal life.

I CAN LEARN

There is only one way to God. Jesus is the only way. Color the STOP red. Color the YIELD yellow. Circle the sign that is the only way to God.

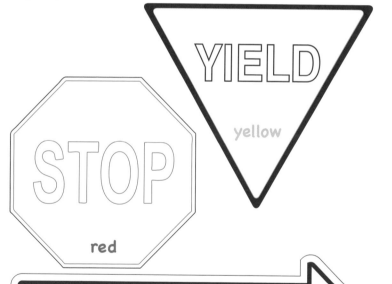

YIELD

yellow

STOP

red

Jesus One Way to God

WAY TO GO!

I CAN PRAY

Ask Jesus to help you tell someone that He is the only Way, the Truth, and the Life.

WEEK #31

229

I CAN KNOW

Jesus lives in heaven now, but when you believe in Jesus, He sends the Holy Spirit to help you obey God.

I CAN LEARN

Did you know God is 3 persons in 1. God is the Father, the Son (Jesus), and the Holy Spirit, our helper. Circle the group that matches the number.

3

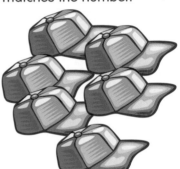

1

I CAN PRAY

Thank Jesus for the Holy Spirit and His help in obeying.

WEEK #32

230

John 14:27

MONDAY

Jesus doesn't want you to be scared or worried. Jesus wants you to trust Him. He cares for you from heaven.

Draw a line underneath the picture that does not belong in each row.

WEEK #32

Ask Jesus to help you not be afraid, but to trust Him all the time.

231

THE BIBLE SAYS

John 15:10-11

TUESDAY

Jesus has a joyful life because He obeys God, His Father. He wants everyone to have a joyful life.

When you obey God, you will have a joyful life. Draw a △ around the picture of the child that has a joyful life.

Thank God for loving you and making you joyful.

WEEK #32

232

WEDNESDAY

Jesus wants you to love others. This is one of His commandments, or rules, you must obey if you follow Him.

Color each heart to finish the pattern.

Ask God to help you obey Him by loving others.

233

I CAN KNOW

The Holy Spirit helps you know what is right and what is wrong. He makes you feel sad when you do wrong things. He makes you feel good when you do what is right.

I CAN LEARN

When you obey God, you should feel happy inside. Draw a ———— from the picture to the correct face.

I CAN PRAY

Ask God to help you listen to the Holy Spirit, your helper, to know what is right and wrong.

WEEK #32

234

FRIDAY

I CAN KNOW

The disciples did not understand what Jesus was saying. He was trying to tell them that soon He was going to die but come alive again. After that Jesus was going to return to heaven to live with God, His Father.

I CAN LEARN

Write a 1 beside what happened first. Write a 2 beside what happened next. Write a 3 beside what happened last.

I CAN PRAY

Thank Jesus for taking the punishment for your sin.

WEEK #32

235

When you pray you talk to God. Jesus says you can ask God for anything, and He will give you what is best for you.

I CAN LEARN

Thank God for hearing and answering prayer. Draw a line from 1 to 13.

WAY TO GO!

I CAN PRAY

WEEK #32

Tell God thank you for hearing and answering your prayer.

SUNDAY

Jesus tells you that eternal life (living forever in heaven) comes from knowing and believing God and Jesus; what they said and what they did.

Believe starts with the beginning sound B. Trace the letter B, and then draw a line from the B to the pictures that start with the letter sound B.

WEEK # 33

Ask Jesus to help you know Him better.

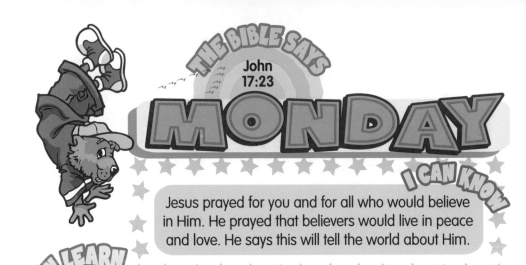

I CAN KNOW

Jesus prayed for you and for all who would believe in Him. He prayed that believers would live in peace and love. He says this will tell the world about Him.

I CAN LEARN

Color the picture of the children at church.

Old Testament   Bible Lesson

I CAN PRAY

Ask God to help you tell others about Him by your actions and your words.

WEEK #33

238

TUESDAY

Jesus was arrested in the garden where He had been praying. God had a plan to save you from your sins through Jesus, His Son.

Jesus wanted to do this for you because He loves you. Draw a line from the soldiers to Jesus.

Thank Jesus for wanting to die for your sin.

WEEK # 33

239

WEDNESDAY

I CAN KNOW

Jesus was accused of doing wrong, but He told the truth and said He did things the right way. Jesus is perfect and could not do wrong.

I CAN LEARN

You should always tell the truth, too. Circle the things in the bottom picture that are different.

I CAN PRAY

Ask God to help you always tell the truth.

John
18:28

THURSDAY

I CAN KNOW

The Jews who arrested Jesus wanted to look like good people. They tried to follow all the rules with their actions, but their hearts were not good.

I CAN LEARN

Jesus wants your heart to be good first, and then your actions will be, too. Draw a line under the biggest one. Color the hearts when you are finished.

I CAN PRAY

Pray for a good heart, filled with Jesus to guide your actions.

WEEK #33

241

John 19:4-5

FRIDAY

I CAN KNOW

Pilate, the judge, could not find anything Jesus had done wrong. It was God's plan for Jesus to suffer and die for your sin. To suffer means to have pain. Jesus felt pain when they called Him names, beat Him and made Him wear a crown of thorns.

I CAN LEARN

The word suffer starts with the letter sound S. Find the hidden S in the picture. Write the letter S on the line.

I CAN PRAY

Thank Jesus for suffering for you.

WEEK #33

242

I CAN KNOW

Even though Pilate found no wrong in Jesus, He did what the crowd wanted. He did what was wrong; He let them kill Jesus.

I CAN LEARN

Draw an **X** over the pictures of things you would not do even if your friends were doing it.

WAY TO GO!

WEEK #33

I CAN PRAY

Ask God to help you do what is right, even when others want you to do what is wrong.

John
19:30

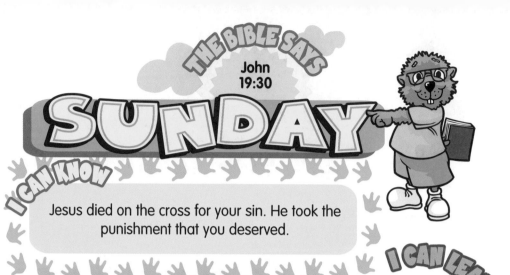

SUNDAY

Jesus died on the cross for your sin. He took the punishment that you deserved.

Color the cross as a reminder of what Jesus did for you.

WEEK #34

Thank Jesus for taking your punishment for sin.

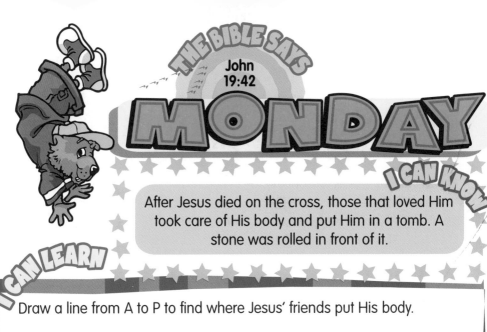

After Jesus died on the cross, those that loved Him took care of His body and put Him in a tomb. A stone was rolled in front of it.

Draw a line from A to P to find where Jesus' friends put His body.

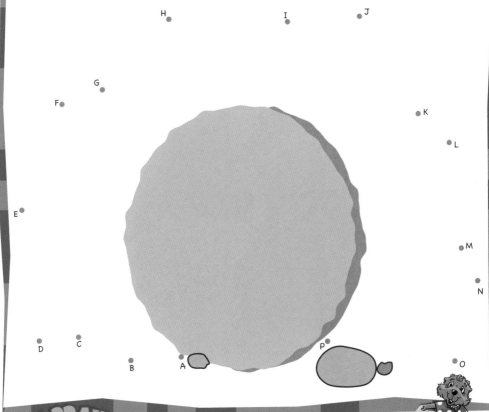

Tell God thank you for friends who care for you.

245

John 20:1-2

TUESDAY

When Mary went to the tomb, she was surprised to find the tomb empty! Jesus was no longer there. She ran to go tell Peter and John.

Write a 1 below what happened first. Write a 2 below what happened next.

WEEK #34

Praise God. Jesus is risen! Alleluia!

246

WEDNESDAY

I CAN KNOW

Mary did not know that Jesus had risen from the dead. When she was crying by the tomb, Jesus came to her and spoke to her. She then ran to tell others that Jesus was alive!

I CAN LEARN

You need to tell others that Jesus is alive, too. Color the letters in the sun yellow to complete this sentence.

Jesus is

ALIVE

I CAN PRAY

Ask God to help you be like Mary and tell others that Jesus is alive!

WEEK #34

I CAN KNOW

Thomas, one of the disciples, would not believe Jesus was alive until he saw Jesus. Jesus says that you are blessed if you believe what is written in the Bible even though you cannot see Jesus with your eyes.

I CAN LEARN

In the first row, circle what you see with. In the second row, circle what you touch things with.

See

Touch

I CAN PRAY

Ask God to help you believe in Jesus even though you cannot see or touch Him.

WEEK #34

FRIDAY

I CAN KNOW

Jesus cared for His friends before His death and after. They could not catch fish on this night, but when they obeyed Jesus they caught lots of fish.

I CAN LEARN

Jesus takes care of you, too! You need to obey Him like the disciples did. Find the 10 hidden fish in the picture.

I CAN PRAY

Thank Jesus for caring for you. Ask Him to help you obey.

WEEK #34

249

THE BIBLE SAYS

John 21:15

SATURDAY

I CAN KNOW

If you love Jesus you will do things for Him. You will love others, care for others, and help others. This is the message Jesus had for Peter.

I CAN LEARN

Color the heart next to the picture if it shows your love for Jesus.

WAY TO GO!

I CAN PRAY

Ask God to help you do good things for others.

WEEK #34

250

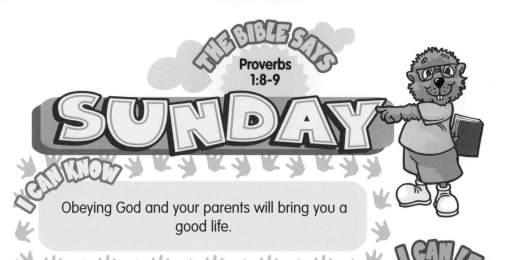

I CAN KNOW

Obeying God and your parents will bring you a good life.

I CAN LEARN

God will help you to obey your parents if you ask Him. Color the picture.

I CAN PRAY

Ask God to help you obey your parents.

WEEK #35

251

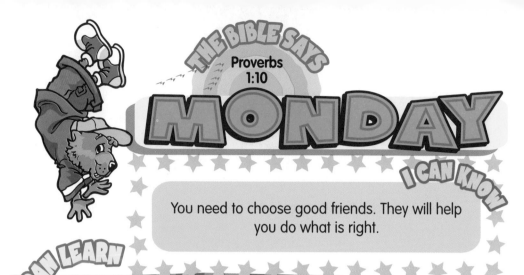

You need to choose good friends. They will help you do what is right.

I CAN LEARN

Draw a ⬤ around the children you would choose to be your friends.

I CAN PRAY

WEEK #35

Ask God to help you choose good friends.

252

I CAN KNOW

When you choose to listen to God, you will not have to be afraid.

I CAN LEARN

You can listen to God by listening to the Bible being read. How many Bibles and ears to you see? Draw a square around the number.

1   2   3

1   2   3

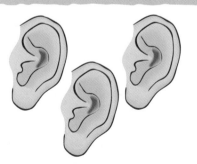

1   2   3

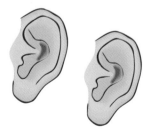

1   2   3

I CAN PRAY

Tell God thank you for His Word, the Bible.

WEEK #35

253

I CAN KNOW

You should search for God's way like you would search for a hidden treasure.

I CAN LEARN

You will be happy if you always search for God's way. ◯ the 10 hidden coins in the picture.

I CAN PRAY

WEEK #35

Ask God to help you follow Him.

You should follow the ways of good people. God will protect you.

I CAN LEARN

Draw a ————— to the group of children you want to follow.

I CAN PRAY

Ask God to help you choose friends wisely.

WEEK #35

FRIDAY

I CAN KNOW

You need to show love to others. When you show love to others, you will be pleasing God.

I CAN LEARN

Draw a ⭕ around the hearts that are the same size. Color the hearts when you are finished.

I CAN PRAY

WEEK #35

Thank God for loving you.

God and your parents correct you when you do wrong because they love you.

Love begins with the letter sound L. Draw a △ around the pictures that begin with the letter sound L. Trace the letter L.

WAY TO GO!

WEEK #35

Thank God for a family that loves you.

257

I CAN KNOW

You don't need to be afraid at night. God will make your sleep sweet.

I CAN LEARN

Draw a ——— from the child sleeping to the pictures that are sweet.

I CAN PRAY

WEEK #36

Ask God to help you not be afraid at night.

258

THE BIBLE SAYS

Proverbs 3:27-28

MONDAY

I CAN KNOW

You should share with others. Sharing shows God's love.

I CAN LEARN

Draw an **X** over the child that is not showing God's love. Draw a ♡ over the child that is showing God's love.

I CAN PRAY

WEEK #36

Ask God to help you share with a happy heart.

259

THE BIBLE SAYS
Proverbs 4:3-4
TUESDAY

Your parents are a gift from God to you. They love you.

You should listen to your parents. They will show you the right way to go. Lead the child to the person to whom he should be listening.

Tell God thank you for your parents.

WEEK #36

260

THE BIBLE SAYS
Proverbs 4:10-12

WEDNESDAY

I CAN KNOW

Obedience is doing what you're told the first time with a happy heart.

I CAN LEARN

You should obey your parents quickly and sweetly. Trace the letter of the beginning sound of each picture.

O   B   E   Y

I CAN PRAY

Ask God to help you obey the first time.

WEEK #36

You should not look at bad things. Keep your heart and mind clean.

I CAN LEARN

Cross out the things that were not found in these verses.

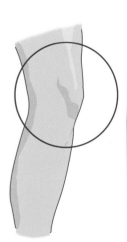

I CAN PRAY

Ask God to help you keep your heart and mind clean.

FRIDAY

I CAN KNOW

Disobeying will always make you unhappy. When you listen and obey, you will be happy.

I CAN LEARN

You should do what is right the first time. Draw a ☐ around the 5 things in the bottom picture that are different.

I CAN PRAY

Ask God to help you do what is right the first time.

WEEK #36

263

God is always watching you. You can't hide from Him.

Draw a blue circle around the set of eyes that are different in each row.

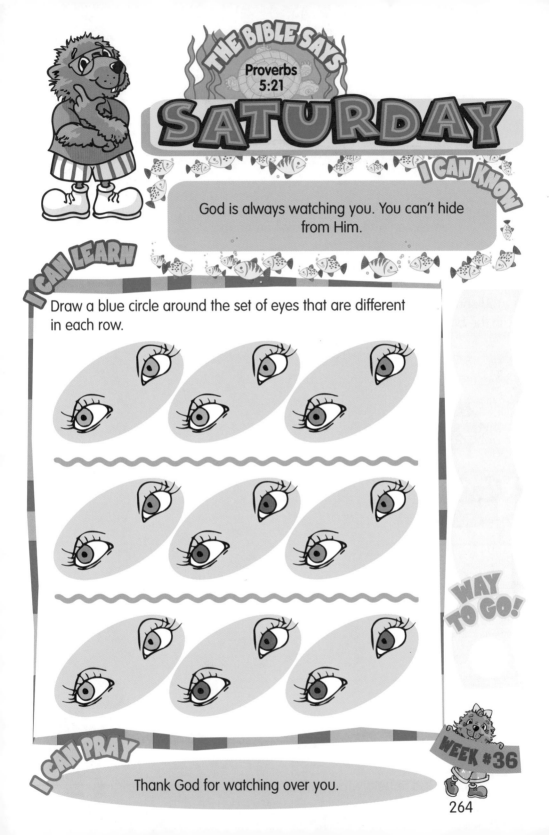

WAY TO GO!

WEEK #36

Thank God for watching over you.

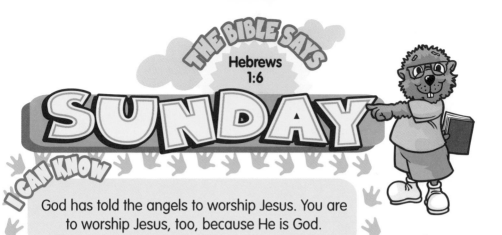

Hebrews 1:6

SUNDAY

I CAN KNOW

God has told the angels to worship Jesus. You are to worship Jesus, too, because He is God.

I CAN LEARN

These children are worshiping Jesus. Circle the 4 things in the bottom picture that are different.

I CAN PRAY

WEEK #37

Worship Jesus by singing a song to Him.

265

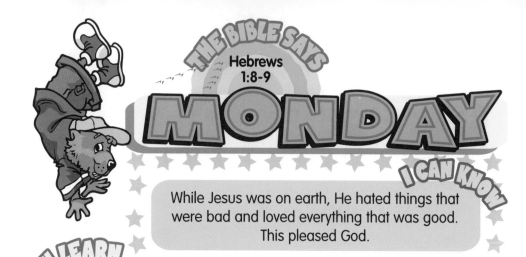

I CAN KNOW

While Jesus was on earth, He hated things that were bad and loved everything that was good. This pleased God.

I CAN LEARN

God hates your sin, but loves the good you do. You sin when you disobey God. Circle the children who are doing good things.

I CAN PRAY

WEEK #37

Ask God to help you do good things that please Him.

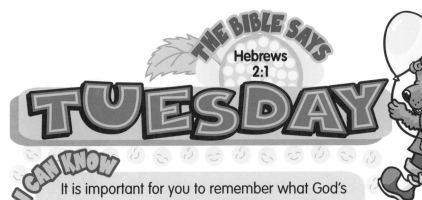

I CAN KNOW

It is important for you to remember what God's Word says. That way you will know right from wrong.

I CAN LEARN

Draw a ——————— to match the opposites.

Wrong   Right

I CAN PRAY

Ask God to help you remember the things you are taught from His Word.

WEEK #37

267

THE BIBLE SAYS

Hebrews 2:14

WEDNESDAY

Jesus became a person just like you, so He could die for your sins and destroy the devil and his power.

Jesus has the power to destroy the devil. Draw a line from A to L.

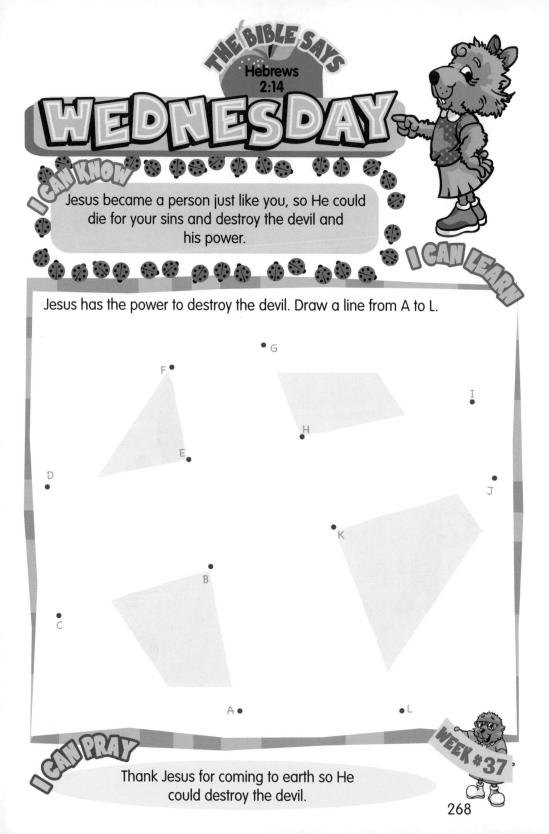

Thank Jesus for coming to earth so He could destroy the devil.

268

I CAN KNOW

Jesus and Moses were faithful to God. You are to be faithful, too. This means that God can trust you to obey Him.

I CAN LEARN

Trace the letters to find out who obeyed God. Trace the letter M if you obey God.

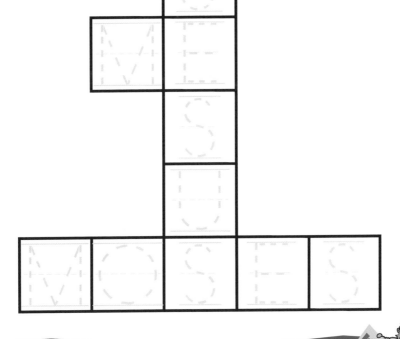

I CAN PRAY

WEEK #37

Pray that you will be faithful to God.

269

FRIDAY

I CAN KNOW

The Bible says you should not have an unbelieving heart. An unbelieving person turns away from God.

I CAN LEARN

If you believe in Jesus as your Savior from sin, you will have a happy heart. Draw an X on the hearts that do not match the clues. Circle the correct heart.

The heart is red.
The heart has a happy face.
The heart has a line underneath it.

I CAN PRAY

If you believe in Jesus as your Savior, thank God that you have a believing heart. If you are unsure, ask God to help you believe.

WEEK #37

I CAN KNOW

If you believe in God and ask Jesus to be your Savior, you will enter heaven someday. You do not want to live apart from God.

I CAN LEARN

Believe begins with the letter sound B. Color the squares with the letter B in them blue.

START	B	H	Q	L	R	H
	B	B	M	B	B	B
	N	B	B	B	B	B
	F	L	A	D	T	B
	G	R	P	E	S	B

HEAVEN

WAY TO GO!

WEEK # 37

I CAN PRAY

Pray that you and all those you love will believe in Jesus.

271

THE BIBLE SAYS

Hebrews 4:9-10

SUNDAY

I CAN KNOW

You should rest on Sunday from your work and worship God.

I CAN LEARN

You go to church on Sunday to worship God. Draw a ——— from 1 to 11.

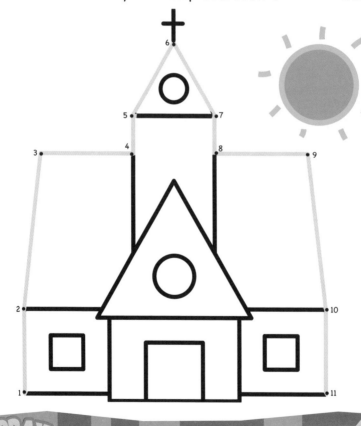

I CAN PRAY

Tell God thank you for the rest He gives you from work to worship Him.

WEEK #38

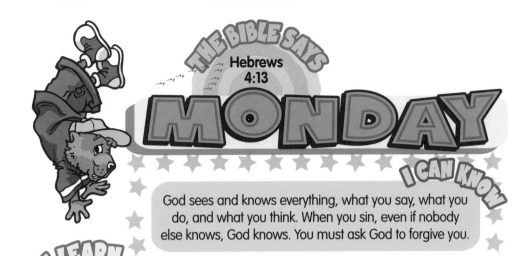

Hebrews
4:13

MONDAY

I CAN KNOW

God sees and knows everything, what you say, what you do, and what you think. When you sin, even if nobody else knows, God knows. You must ask God to forgive you.

I CAN LEARN

You can never hide from God. Draw a circle around the children that are hiding from their friend.

I CAN PRAY

Ask God to help you do the right thing, even if nobody sees you.

WEEK #38

273

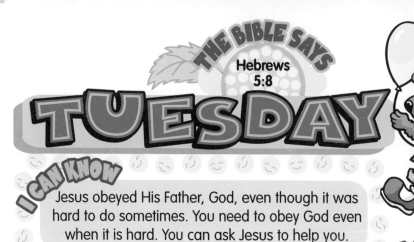

I CAN KNOW

Jesus obeyed His Father, God, even though it was hard to do sometimes. You need to obey God even when it is hard. You can ask Jesus to help you.

I CAN LEARN

Draw a line from the child who needs to ask Jesus' help to obey, to the same child who is asking for Jesus' help.

I CAN PRAY

Ask Jesus to help you obey even when it is hard to do.

WEEK #38

274

THE BIBLE SAYS

Hebrews 5:13-14

WEDNESDAY

I CAN KNOW

As you learn more of God's Word, you grow from a baby Christian to a grown-up Christian. As a grown-up Christian, you will know right from wrong, and you will want to choose the right way.

I CAN LEARN

Draw a ———— to match the opposites.

I CAN PRAY

Ask God to help you learn His Word and make good choices.

WEEK #38

THURSDAY

I CAN KNOW

Ground that is soft is useful for growing good plants. God wants you to be useful for Him. You should behave in ways that show others that you love Him.

I CAN LEARN

Draw a circle around the picture that does not belong in each row.

I CAN PRAY

WEEK #38

Ask God to help you show others that you love Him.

276

FRIDAY

Sometimes God asks you to patiently wait for good things. He always keeps His promises, so you should wait happily.

The word promise begins with the letter sound P. Circle the picture that goes with the first one.

Pie

Pig

Pillow

WEEK #38

Tell God thank you for always keeping His promises to you.

I CAN KNOW

God is perfect. He cannot lie. You can believe and trust what His Word says and the promises He makes.

I CAN LEARN

You can always trust God's Word, the Bible. It is true. Say the picture words. Circle the picture word that begins with the same sound.

Tr truck

U umbrella

S sun

T top

WAY TO GO!

I CAN PRAY

Thank God that you can always trust Him.

WEEK #38

278

THE BIBLE SAYS

Hebrews 7:9

SUNDAY

I CAN KNOW

Tithe is money you give to God in your church offering to thank Him for what He has given you and to help your church.

I CAN LEARN

You may not have any money, but you can help your church in other ways. Draw a square around the children who are helping their church.

Old Testament   Bible Lesson

I CAN PRAY

Ask God to help you be a helper at church.

WEEK #39

279

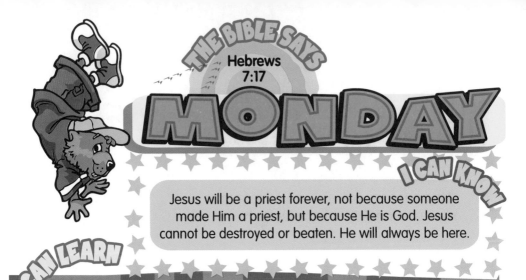

I CAN KNOW

Jesus will be a priest forever, not because someone made Him a priest, but because He is God. Jesus cannot be destroyed or beaten. He will always be here.

I CAN LEARN

You can always know that Jesus will be with you. He loves you very much. Write your name in the blank.

Jesus loves
_____!

I CAN PRAY

Praise Jesus for being so great!

WEEK #39

TUESDAY

I CAN KNOW

Before Jesus took the punishment for sins by dying on the cross, people tried to get closer to God by obeying laws.

I CAN LEARN

Laws cannot save you from your sin. Jesus is the only way you can get to God. ⭕ the only way to get to God.

LAW JESUS

I CAN PRAY

Tell God thank you for giving you Jesus.

WEEK #39

WEDNESDAY

I CAN KNOW

Jesus is able to give you eternal life if you believe in Him. You can live forever with Him in heaven.

I CAN LEARN

Jesus is always ready to hear your prayer and forgive you. Draw a —— from the child to HEAVEN.

HEAVEN

I CAN PRAY

WEEK #39

Do you need to ask forgiveness for your sins?
Ask Jesus, and then thank Him for forgiving you.

282

THURSDAY

I CAN KNOW

Jesus is sitting next to God in heaven. He is there talking to God for you.

I CAN LEARN

Color the picture.

I CAN PRAY

Thank Jesus for all He does for you.

WEEK #39

FRIDAY

I CAN KNOW

God wants His law, His Word, on your mind and in your heart. You can do this by memorizing Bible verses. Then you will always know what God says.

I CAN LEARN

Draw a line under the set that has more.

I CAN PRAY

Ask God to help you memorize Bible verses.

WEEK #39

284

THE BIBLE SAYS

Hebrews 9:7

SATURDAY

I CAN KNOW

Before Jesus came to earth to die, a priest would pray to God and bring a sacrifice for the people asking for forgiveness of their sins. Because of what Jesus did for you, you can ask God for forgiveness. You do not need someone else to do it for you.

I CAN LEARN

Draw a ———— from A to L. Color the picture when you are finished.

WAY TO GO!

WEEK #39

I CAN PRAY

Tell Jesus thank you for dying on the cross for your sin.

285

SUNDAY

I CAN KNOW

Jesus died and He bled for your sins. He became the sacrifice that pleased God, which gives you life forever when you believe.

I CAN LEARN

Draw a ———— from each picture to its shadow.

I CAN PRAY

WEEK #40

Tell Jesus thank you for dying for your sins.

THE BIBLE SAYS

Hebrews 9:22

MONDAY

I CAN KNOW

God's law says that blood has to be shed for sins to be forgiven. Jesus did this for you.

I CAN LEARN

Jesus loves you very much. He took the punishment for your sin. Draw a line from the children to the one who can forgive their sin.

I CAN PRAY

Tell Jesus thank you for loving you so much.

WEEK #40

287

THE BIBLE SAYS
Hebrews 9:28
TUESDAY

Jesus is coming again. You need to tell others how Jesus forgives their sin.

I CAN LEARN

Draw a circle around the children who are telling others about Jesus.

I CAN PRAY

Ask Jesus to help you tell others about Him.

WEEK #40

288

WEDNESDAY

I CAN KNOW

Jesus only had to die once, and His blood covers all your sins all the time.

I CAN LEARN

Draw a line from 1 to 6. Then draw a line from A to B. Next, draw a line from 1 to 4. Color the cross red to remind you of Jesus shedding His blood for your sin.

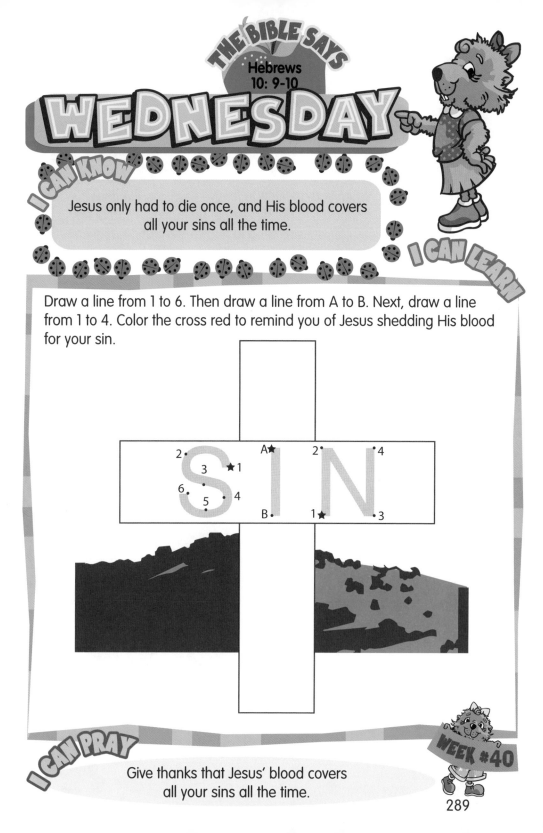

I CAN PRAY

Give thanks that Jesus' blood covers all your sins all the time.

WEEK #40

289

I CAN KNOW

When you ask God to forgive your sins, He does. God chooses to not remember them. When somebody hurts you, you need to forgive them and love them.

I CAN LEARN

Draw a line to match the child who is forgiving.

I CAN PRAY

Pray for someone who has hurt you. Ask God to help you forgive them and forget what they have done to you.

WEEK #40

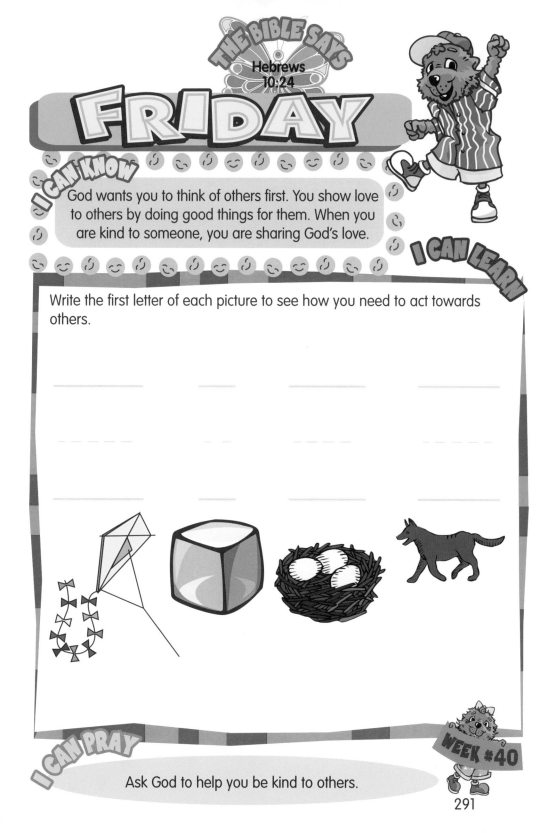

THE BIBLE SAYS
Hebrews 10:24

FRIDAY

I CAN KNOW

God wants you to think of others first. You show love to others by doing good things for them. When you are kind to someone, you are sharing God's love.

I CAN LEARN

Write the first letter of each picture to see how you need to act towards others.

I CAN PRAY

Ask God to help you be kind to others.

WEEK #40

291

God will punish those who do wrong and do not ask forgiveness. You do not need to hurt someone who has hurt you.

I CAN LEARN

Color the letters to discover who will punish those who do wrong.

1 = red
2 = orange
3 = blue

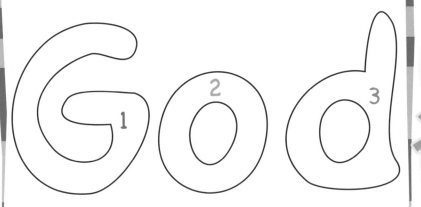

WAY TO GO!

I CAN PRAY

Think about your behavior this week. What do you need to ask forgiveness for?

WEEK #40

292

SUNDAY

I CAN KNOW

Sometimes you do not get rewarded for your good behavior. Don't be upset. Keep doing what is good because God will reward you someday.

I CAN LEARN

Circle the number of crowns in each row. Color the jewels.

1 2 3 4 5

1 2 3 4 5

1 2 3 4 5

1 2 3 4 5

I CAN PRAY

Ask God to help you do what is right even if nobody knows.

WEEK # 41

MONDAY

In order to please God, you must have faith in Him. Are you pleasing God by believing in Jesus?

The word faith begins with the letter sound f. Color the pictures that begin with the letter sound f. Write the letter F.

Ask God to help you believe everything you read in your Bible.

WEEK # 41

I CAN KNOW

It had never rained before the flood, yet Noah believed what God told Him and obeyed by building the ark. You can always believe God.

I CAN LEARN

Help the animals find the ark. Find the pattern. Color the rocks to finish the path.

I CAN PRAY

Ask God to help you believe Him even when you don't understand.

WEEK # 41

WEDNESDAY

Abraham believed that God would keep His promise of giving him a big family, even when God asked Abraham to sacrifice his son, Isaac.

Because Abraham trusted and believed, God sent a ram for him to sacrifice instead. Color the ram hiding in the bushes.

WEEK # 41

Ask God to help you trust Him even when you have to do something hard.

I CAN KNOW

Moses' parents believed that God would protect him, even though the king was very evil. They hid baby Moses in a basket.

I CAN LEARN

Draw a line under the picture that is different in each row.

I CAN PRAY

WEEK # 41

Thank God for always protecting you.

297

FRIDAY

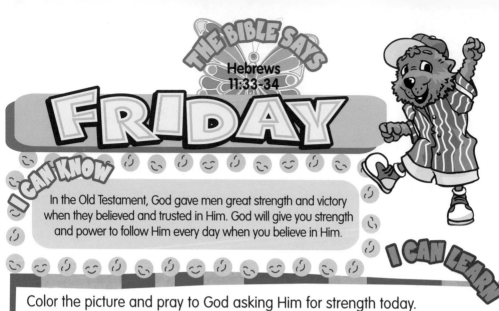

In the Old Testament, God gave men great strength and victory when they believed and trusted in Him. God will give you strength and power to follow Him every day when you believe in Him.

I CAN LEARN

Color the picture and pray to God asking Him for strength today.

God's Strength

I CAN PRAY

Thank God for the strength He gives you to say no to sin and yes to obeying Him.

I CAN KNOW

Sometimes bad things happen to people who love God. When bad things happen, you need to keep believing and trusting in God. He will take care of you and reward you in heaven for your troubles.

I CAN LEARN

Color the first crown blue. Circle the third crown.

Color the fourth crown purple. Draw a line under the second crown.

WAY TO GO!

I CAN PRAY

Pray that when bad things happen, you will keep believing and trusting God.

WEEK # 41

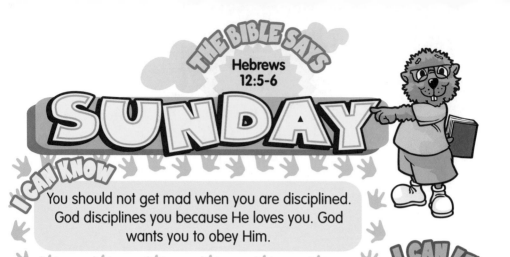

I CAN KNOW

You should not get mad when you are disciplined. God disciplines you because He loves you. God wants you to obey Him.

I CAN LEARN

You should obey your parents and teachers. Draw a line from the word obey to the people you should obey.

Obey

I CAN PRAY

WEEK #42

Thank God for loving you and disciplining you.

MONDAY

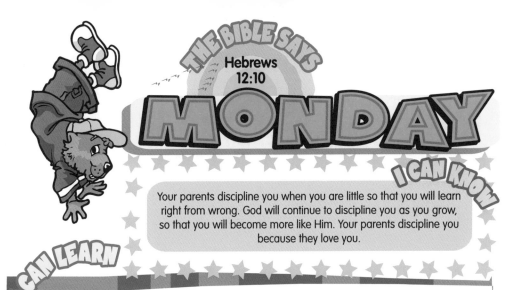

Your parents discipline you when you are little so that you will learn right from wrong. God will continue to discipline you as you grow, so that you will become more like Him. Your parents discipline you because they love you.

I CAN LEARN

How many of these can you find in the picture? Count and write the number.

I CAN PRAY

Ask God to help you obey the first time with a happy heart.

WEEK #42

301

I CAN KNOW

God welcomes you into His kingdom, heaven. Your name can be written in heaven. You must say that you are a sinner, believe that Jesus died for your sins, confess your sin and ask Jesus to forgive you.

I CAN LEARN

If you have accepted Jesus as your Savior, write your name in the blank. If you want to know more about Jesus as your Savior, ask your parent or a teacher at church.

_____

_____

_____

I CAN PRAY

Thank God for His great love for you.

WEEK #42

302

THE BIBLE SAYS
Hebrews 12:28
WEDNESDAY

Heaven cannot be destroyed. If you have accepted Jesus as your Savior, you will always have a home there. You should show God your thanks by serving Him.

I CAN LEARN

Draw a ———— underneath the children that are serving God.

I CAN PRAY

WEEK #42

Thank God for your forever home in heaven.

303

I CAN KNOW

Jesus will never change. Who He is, what He said, and what He did will never change. He will always love and care for you and forgive your sin.

I CAN LEARN

These things change. Write 1, 2, and 3 to show the order.

I CAN PRAY

Thank Jesus for never changing; for always loving you and caring for you.

WEEK #42

304

THE BIBLE SAYS

Hebrews 13:14

FRIDAY

Nothing on earth will last forever. The city to come that will last forever is heaven. You can look forward to this wonderful place.

I CAN LEARN

Draw a ————— from the children to heaven.

HEAVEN

I CAN PRAY

WEEK #42

Praise God for creating a city that will be forever, heaven.

I CAN KNOW

You need to do good things and tell what you know about Jesus with others. This pleases Jesus when you share Him.

I CAN LEARN

Look at the picture. Draw the missing parts.

WAY TO GO!

I CAN PRAY

Ask God to help you tell others about Jesus.

WEEK #42

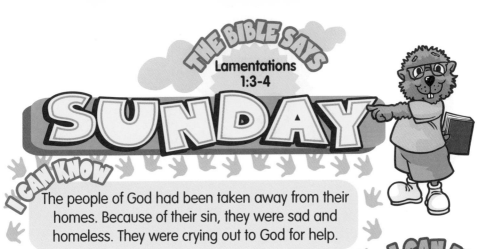

I CAN KNOW

The people of God had been taken away from their homes. Because of their sin, they were sad and homeless. They were crying out to God for help.

I CAN LEARN

When you sin, you can ask out to God to forgive you. Write the letter of the beginning sound of each picture.

The people of God had no place to

I CAN PRAY

Pray for someone who needs to know about Jesus.

WEEK #43

307

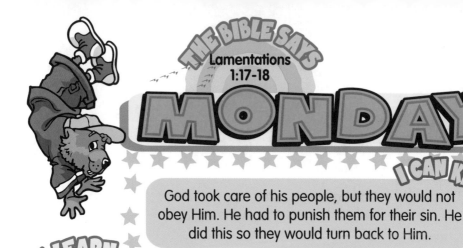

I CAN KNOW

God took care of his people, but they would not obey Him. He had to punish them for their sin. He did this so they would turn back to Him.

I CAN LEARN

God takes care of you, too. You need to obey God. Draw a line from 1 to 5. Next draw a line from 6 to 9. Then draw a line from 10 to 13.

You should obey

I CAN PRAY

Ask God to help you obey Him.

WEEK #43

I CAN KNOW

Because God is without sin, He must punish it.
God did not want to see His people hurting.

I CAN LEARN

God punishes sin to turn you back to Him. Draw a line to help God's people go back to whom they should obey.

GOD

SELF

I CAN PRAY

Pray for your brother, sister or friend.

WEEK #43

309

WEDNESDAY

The people began to cry out to God for help. They knew that He was the only One who could save them.

He can save you, too. All you have to do is ask. Draw a ◯ around what you would use to call out to God.

Ask God to help you with something today.

God loves you so much, more than you can count or imagine.

I CAN LEARN

Draw a ◯ around the group that is greater.

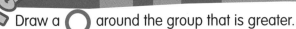

God's love   Your love

I CAN PRAY

Pray for someone who needs your love.

WEEK #43

FRIDAY

I CAN KNOW

God will hear your call for help. He is always with you.

I CAN LEARN

Find the five hidden ears in the picture. Draw a ☐ around them.

I CAN PRAY

Thank God for always hearing you when you talk to Him.

WEEK #43

312

I CAN KNOW

Sin takes away your joy and happiness. You can ask God to forgive you, and He will make your heart joyful again.

I CAN LEARN

Draw a picture of something that makes you happy.

WAY TO GO!

I CAN PRAY

Praise God for your family.

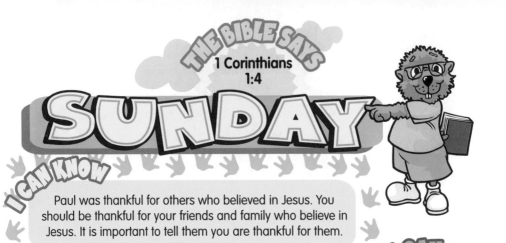

1 Corinthians 1:4

SUNDAY

I CAN KNOW

Paul was thankful for others who believed in Jesus. You should be thankful for your friends and family who believe in Jesus. It is important to tell them you are thankful for them.

I CAN LEARN

Circle the people you are thankful for.

I CAN PRAY

WEEK #44

Thank God for all the people in your life who believe in Jesus.

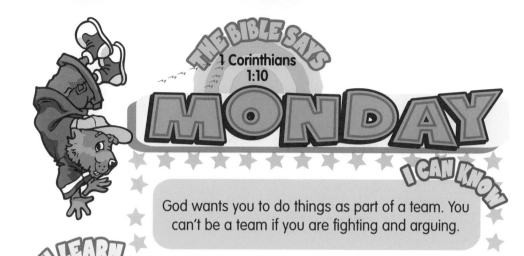

I CAN KNOW

God wants you to do things as part of a team. You can't be a team if you are fighting and arguing.

I CAN LEARN

Start at home plate and run the bases. Write the letters in the blank as you tag each base.

When I _ _ _ _ _ others I am a team player!

I CAN PRAY

WEEK #44

Ask God to help you get along with others.

315

I CAN KNOW

Many people do not understand that Jesus died on the cross for their sin. It doesn't make sense to them. Other people do understand and believe. They know Jesus' awesome power to save them from their sin.

I CAN LEARN

You need to tell others how Jesus will forgive their sin. Draw a line under the place where you can tell others about Jesus.

FRESH VEGGIES

I CAN PRAY

Ask Jesus to help others believe in His power to save them from their sin.

WEEK #44

316

1 Corinthians 2:4-5

WEDNESDAY

Paul did not use big words when he told people about Jesus. He made it simple, so they would understand about Jesus. You can tell others about Jesus too, even if you cannot read or write.

You can tell others about Jesus when you are at the playground. Draw a line to each thing in the picture.

Ask Jesus to help you tell others about Him.

I CAN KNOW

You can't see, hear, or know what God will choose to have happen in your life as you grow up. However, God gives you the Holy Spirit to help you know what God wants and to help you make good choices.

I CAN LEARN

Draw in the missing parts.

I CAN PRAY

Thank God for the Holy Spirit.

WEEK #44

FRIDAY

When you tell your friends about Jesus, it is as if you are planting a seed. When others keep telling them about Jesus, they are watering that seed. God helps that seed to grow.

Match the names on the left side with the part they have in telling others about Jesus.

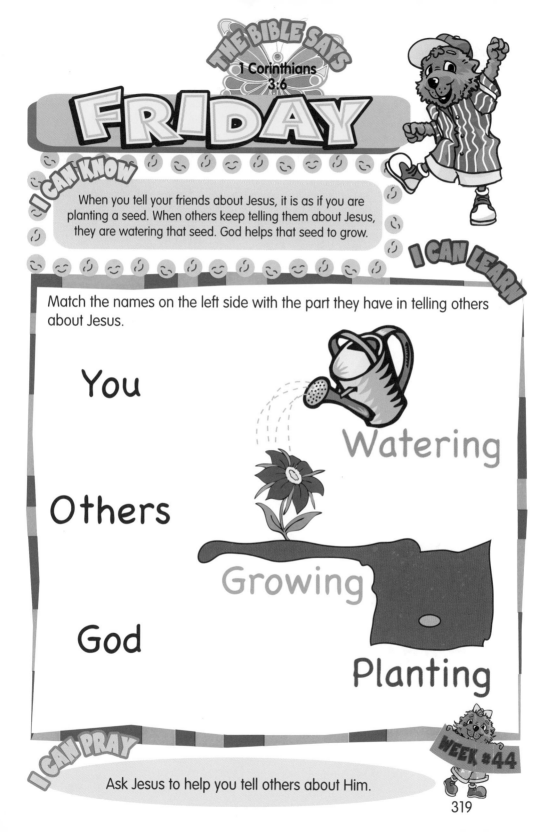

You

Watering

Others

Growing

God

Planting

Ask Jesus to help you tell others about Him.

1 Corinthians 3:13-14

SATURDAY

God wants you to do everything with a happy heart. Someday God will look at all the things you have done. If you had a happy heart when you did them, God will reward you. God won't count those things done with an unhappy heart.

I CAN LEARN

O the picture that is above the others. Draw an X on the picture that is below the others.

WAY TO GO!

WEEK #44

I CAN PRAY

Ask God to help you have a happy heart in everything you do.

SUNDAY

I CAN KNOW

When you accept Jesus as your Savior, He makes His home in your heart. Because Jesus lives in you, He wants you to take care of your body.

I CAN LEARN

Draw a line under the things that are good for your body. Draw an X over the things that are bad for your body.

WEEK #45

I CAN PRAY

Ask God to help you take good care of your body.

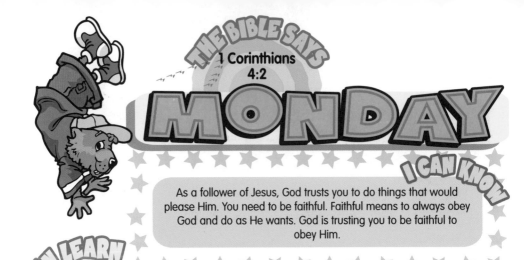

I CAN KNOW

As a follower of Jesus, God trusts you to do things that would please Him. You need to be faithful. Faithful means to always obey God and do as He wants. God is trusting you to be faithful to obey Him.

I CAN LEARN

Trace the word obey. Draw a line from the word obey to the things that you can do to obey God.

I can God.

I CAN PRAY

Pray that you will be faithful and that you will always obey God.

322

THE BIBLE SAYS

1 Corinthians 4:16

TUESDAY

I CAN KNOW

Paul was a faithful follower of Jesus. He obeyed God and did many good things for God. He encouraged others to act as he did. You should follow the examples of people who love God. They can be people in the Bible, people in your family, or people in your church.

I CAN LEARN

Think of one person you know who loves God. Draw their picture in the frame.

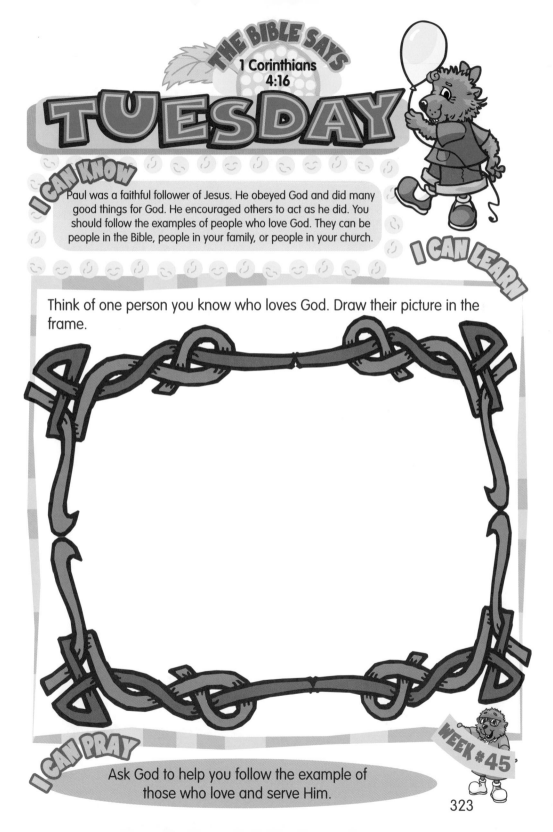

I CAN PRAY

Ask God to help you follow the example of those who love and serve Him.

WEEK #45

323

THE BIBLE SAYS
1 Corinthians 5:2

WEDNESDAY

I CAN KNOW

The people were not sorry or sad over a sin that another person had done. Instead they were proud and happy. Sin upsets God. It should make you sorry and sad when you sin or see another person sin.

I CAN LEARN

When you sin you need to tell Jesus that you are sorry. The words sin and sorry begin with the letter sound S. Draw a line above the pictures that begin with the letter sound S. Write the letter S.

I CAN PRAY

WEEK #45

Ask God to help you feel sad when you see others sin.

324

You are dirty with sin. You can become clean by accepting Jesus as your Savior. Tell Jesus you are a sinner, that you are sorry and that you believe Jesus died for your sins.

I CAN LEARN

Dirty and clean are opposites. Draw a ———— to match the opposites.

old

boy

open

dirty

girl

clean

new

closed

I CAN PRAY

Thank God for making sinners clean through Jesus.

WEEK #45

FRIDAY

I CAN KNOW

Your body belongs to God. You need to use your body to honor God.

I CAN LEARN

Draw a line from each body part to how you can honor God with it.

I CAN PRAY

Ask God to help you use your body to honor Him.

WEEK #45

326

God has made you different from others. He has made you special. You can do things that others cannot. This is a gift from God.

I CAN LEARN

Draw a line from the gift box to the thing you like to do for others.

WAY TO GO!

WEEK #45

I CAN PRAY

Tell God thank you for making you special.

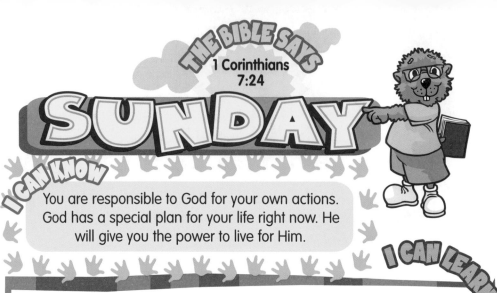

I CAN KNOW

You are responsible to God for your own actions. God has a special plan for your life right now. He will give you the power to live for Him.

I CAN LEARN

Power begins with the letter sound P. Draw a ———— from the pictures that begin with the letter sound P to the letter P.

P

I CAN PRAY

Tell God thank you for giving you power to live for Him.

WEEK #46

328

1 Corinthians 7:35

MONDAY

God gives you rules in the Bible. He gives you rules for your good, so you can live the right way.

I CAN LEARN

Draw a line from 2 to 10. Count by twos. Trace the word Bible.

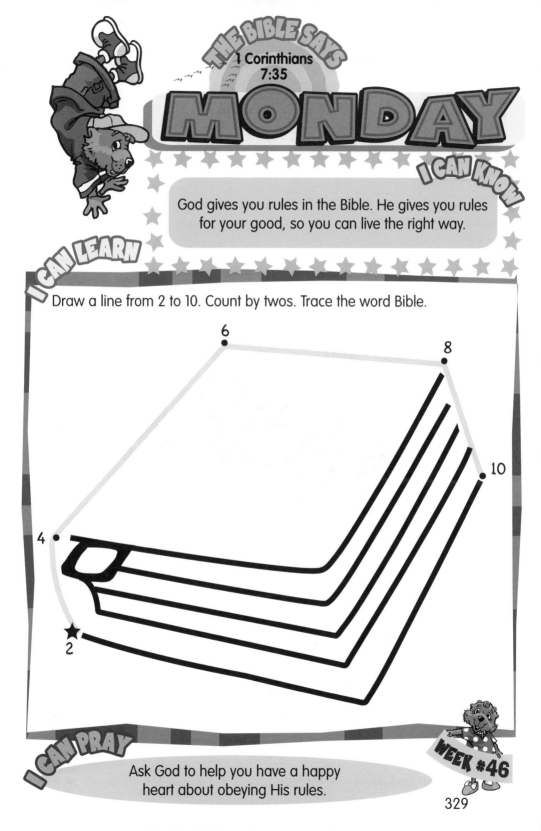

I CAN PRAY

Ask God to help you have a happy heart about obeying His rules.

WEEK #46

THE BIBLE SAYS
1 Corinthians 8:6

TUESDAY

I CAN KNOW

There is one God. There is one Savior, Jesus. He is the One who saves you from your sin.

I CAN LEARN

Circle everything there is only one of.

God

Jesus

I CAN PRAY

WEEK #46

Tell God thank you for being the only God.

330

WEDNESDAY

I CAN KNOW

God gives you many things. Sometimes you have to share those things to help other people.

I CAN LEARN

Draw a ———— underneath the things you can share with others.

I CAN PRAY

Ask God to help you be able to share your things with others.

WEEK #46

THURSDAY

I CAN KNOW

Paul was a missionary. He shared the Good News of Jesus with others. Missionaries go to all parts of the world telling others about Jesus. God wants you to help the missionaries. He wants you to pray for missionaries and to give money or other things they need.

I CAN LEARN

Draw a square around the things you can to do for missionaries.

I CAN PRAY

Ask God to keep missionaries safe as they tell others about Him.

WEEK #46

FRIDAY

When you run a race, you run as fast as you can to win the prize. You do your best. God wants you to do your best as His follower. He will reward you.

Draw a line from the runners to their prize.

Tell God you want to do your best as His follower.

WEEK #46

God does not want you to love anything more than you love Him. If you love something more than God, it is an idol. This is a sin.

I CAN LEARN

Color the things that you could love more than God.

WAY TO GO!

I CAN PRAY

Ask God to help you love Him more than anything.

WEEK #46

334

THE BIBLE SAYS
1 Corinthians
10:12

SUNDAY

I CAN KNOW

Do not think there are some sins you would never do. Every day you must make the choice to obey God.

I CAN LEARN

Draw a ——————from the child to the choice he needs to make.

WEEK #47

I CAN PRAY

Ask God to help you make good choices that please Him.

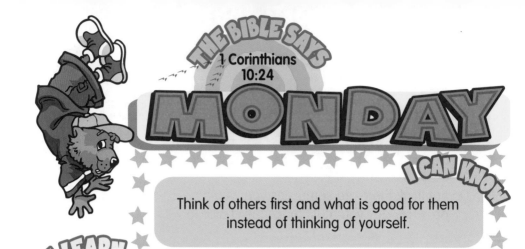

THE BIBLE SAYS

1 Corinthians
10:24

MONDAY

I CAN KNOW

Think of others first and what is good for them instead of thinking of yourself.

I CAN LEARN

Circle the things in the bottom picture that are different.

I CAN PRAY

Ask God to help you put others before yourself.

WEEK #47

TUESDAY

I CAN KNOW

Paul knew all about Jesus and followed the God's rules. Paul was a good example to others. You can be a good example by following the example of people who obey God.

I CAN LEARN

Draw a ————— from the children to whom they should be following.

I CAN PRAY

Ask God to help you follow others who obey God.

WEEK #47

337

THE BIBLE SAYS
1 Corinthians 11:18
WEDNESDAY

Paul heard that the people in this church were not getting along. This made Paul and God unhappy.

Draw the face that God makes when He sees you being kind to your friends.

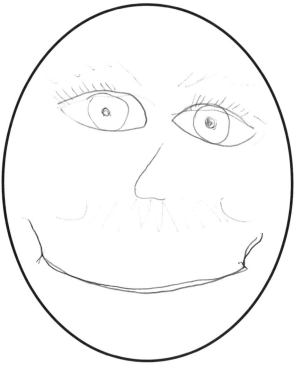

WEEK #47

Ask God to help you be kind to others.

I CAN KNOW

It is not your job to judge other people. When you sin, you need to ask God for forgiveness and try not to do it again.

I CAN LEARN

The words job and judge begin with the letter sound J. Trace the letter J. Write J to finish the picture words.

jelly

I CAN PRAY

Ask God to help you know when you sin.

WEEK #47

339

FRIDAY

I CAN KNOW

When you do things for God, you are serving Him. Make sure that you do your best for God in everything you do.

I CAN LEARN

Draw a line under the one thing you are going to do to serve God this week.

WEEK #47

I CAN PRAY

Tell God that you want to serve Him today and every day.

THE BIBLE SAYS

1 Corinthians 12:17-18

SATURDAY

You are important to God. He made you just the way you are for a special reason. You do not have to be like everybody else.

Circle the picture that does not belong in each row.

Thank God for making you special!

WEEK #47

341

1 Corinthians 12:27

SUNDAY

I CAN KNOW

As a part of God's family, you are important and have a special job to do for God.

I CAN LEARN

Circle the people who have a special job for God.

Old Testament   Bible Lesson

I CAN PRAY

Pray that everyone in God's family will do their best job for Him.

WEEK #48

342

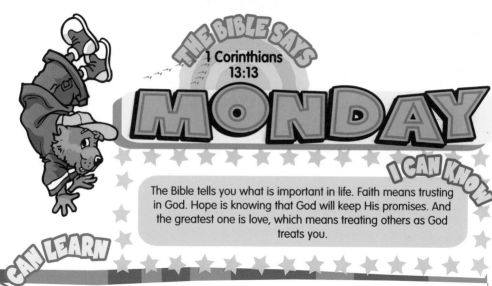

I CAN LEARN

The Bible tells you what is important in life. Faith means trusting in God. Hope is knowing that God will keep His promises. And the greatest one is love, which means treating others as God treats you.

Write in each missing number.

1 2 □ 4

5 6 □ 8

3 4 5 □

7 □ 9 10

I CAN PRAY

Ask God to help you love others.

WEEK #48

343

THE BIBLE SAYS
1 Corinthians 14:3

TUESDAY

You should use the gifts God has given you to share the gospel, and to help to others by your words and your actions.

I CAN LEARN

Circle how many in each row.

4   5   6

4   5   6

4   5   6

4   5   6

I CAN PRAY

WEEK #48

Pray that you will be a help to someone today.

WEDNESDAY

I CAN KNOW

Even as a little person, God has made you so you can do things to help your church. You can help clean up your Sunday school room. You can pick up trash in the hallways. You can pray.

I CAN LEARN

Color the picture of the church using the color key.

☐ = red

▭ = green

◯ = yellow

△ = blue

I CAN PRAY

Pray for your church today.

WEEK #48

You should know very little about evil things. You should know all you can about God's Word.

I CAN LEARN

Say a Scripture memory verse that you have learned to your mom or dad. Color the picture of the Bible.

Holy Bible

I CAN PRAY

Ask God to help you stay away from evil and to learn all you can from His Word.

WEEK #48

FRIDAY

I CAN KNOW

God does not like confusion in the church. He wants His house to be a place of peace. You should know how to behave in church. This way you and others can worship God and learn.

I CAN LEARN

Circle the church that is different.

I CAN PRAY

Ask God to help you sit quietly in church and listen well.

WEEK #48

347

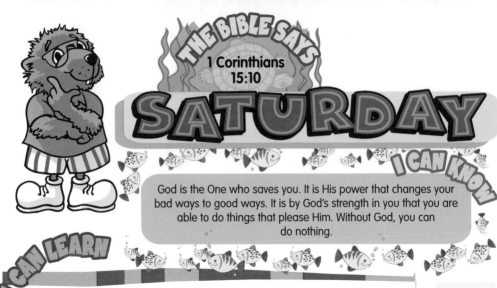

God is the One who saves you. It is His power that changes your bad ways to good ways. It is by God's strength in you that you are able to do things that please Him. Without God, you can do nothing.

I CAN LEARN

Draw a circle around the person who gives you strength.

God

Others

WAY TO GO!

I CAN PRAY

Thank God for helping you to do what is right.

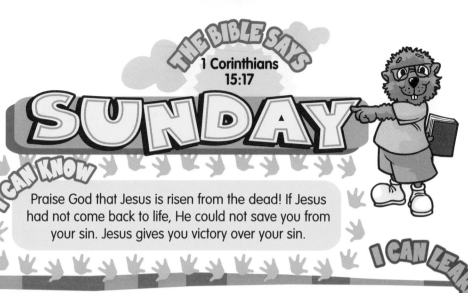

THE BIBLE SAYS

1 Corinthians 15:17

SUNDAY

I CAN KNOW

Praise God that Jesus is risen from the dead! If Jesus had not come back to life, He could not save you from your sin. Jesus gives you victory over your sin.

I CAN LEARN

Victory begins with the letter sound V. Draw a line above the pictures that begin with the letter sound V. Write the letter V.

I CAN PRAY

Praise God that Jesus is alive!

WEEK #49

349

I CAN KNOW

Sin came into the world through Adam. Now everyone sins. The punishment for sin is death being separated from God forever. Jesus died for your sin. You can live with God forever if you believe in what Jesus did for you and ask His forgiveness.

I CAN LEARN

Draw a ———— from A to L. Color the picture.

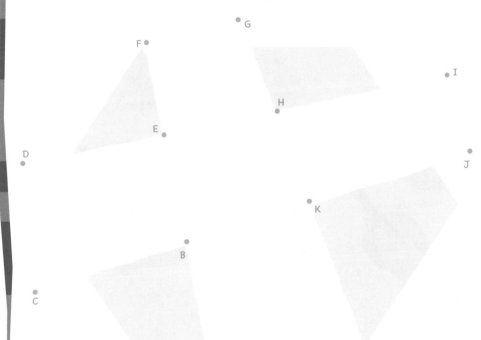

I CAN PRAY

Tell Jesus thank you for dying for your sin.

WEEK #49

350

TUESDAY

I CAN KNOW

God wants you to choose good friends. Friends who do bad things will make you forget God's rules and do bad things too.

I CAN LEARN

Draw a line from the children to whom they should choose for their friends.

I CAN PRAY

Ask God to help you make good friends.

WEEK #49

351

WEDNESDAY

I CAN KNOW

In heaven God will give you a new body. It will never die. It will be strong and beautiful.

I CAN LEARN

Draw a ——— from the children to heaven.

Heaven

I CAN PRAY

Praise God for the wonderful things He has planned for you in heaven.

WEEK #49

352

I CAN KNOW

Jesus is coming back to the earth someday to take all those who believe in Him to heaven. This will happen very quickly.

I CAN LEARN

Write the number 1 beside what will happen first; a number 2 beside what will happen next; and a number 3 beside what will happen last.

I CAN PRAY

Pray for someone who does not believe in Jesus as their Savior.

WEEK #49

353

FRIDAY

Everything you have comes from God. God gives people their jobs, so they can earn money to buy the things they need. By giving some of that money to the offering, you are saying "thank you" to God.

Draw a ——————— under the things that God wants you spend your money on.

Thank God for something He has given you. Ask Him to help you share what you have with Him and others.

THE BIBLE SAYS

1 Corinthians 16:13

SATURDAY

I CAN KNOW

As you wait for Jesus to come back, He wants you to be brave and strong for Him and to never stop believing in Him.

I CAN LEARN

Circle the children that are ready for Jesus to come back.

WAY TO GO!

WEEK #49

I CAN PRAY

Pray that you will be brave and strong for God.

355

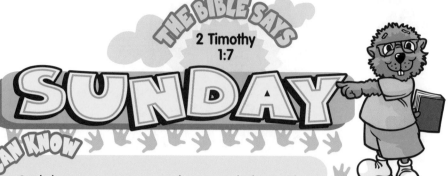

2 Timothy 1:7

SUNDAY

I CAN KNOW

God does not want you to be scared about what others think of you. He will make you strong.

I CAN LEARN

God will help you to love others. Trace the words. Fill in the missing letters by using the clues.

1. S T R O N G

Across:
1. God will make me

_ _ _ _ _ _.

2. God will help me to

_ _ _ _ others.

Down:
1. God does not want me to be

_ _ _ _ _ _.

2. L O V E

I CAN PRAY

Ask God to help you love others and not be scared of what they think of you.

WEEK #50

356

MONDAY

I CAN KNOW

Jesus died on the cross for your sin because He loves you. You cannot be saved by anything you do.

I CAN LEARN

Draw a line from the letter A to the letter L. Color the cross when you are finished.

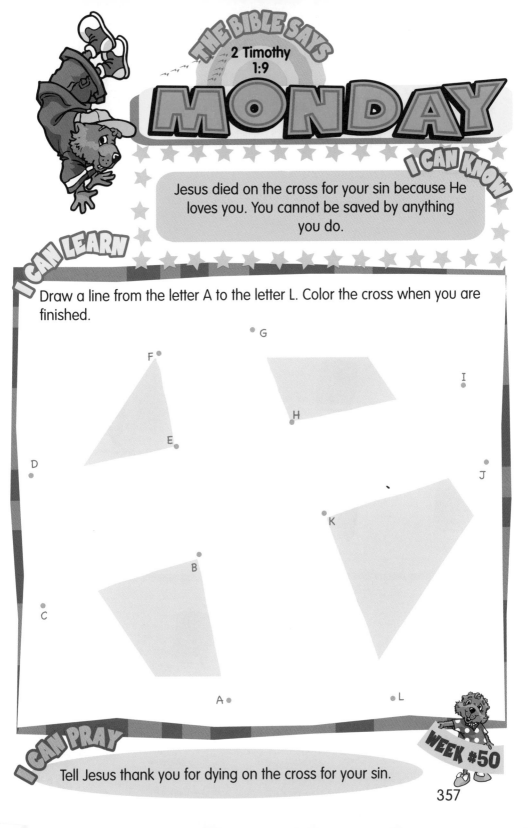

I CAN PRAY

Tell Jesus thank you for dying on the cross for your sin.

WEEK #50

357

THE BIBLE SAYS

2 Timothy 1:14

TUESDAY

God wants you to remember His Word all the time. The best way to do this is to memorize verses.

I CAN LEARN

Draw a circle around the Bibles that are the same size.

I CAN PRAY

WEEK #50

Ask God to help you learn verses from the Bible.

358

WEDNESDAY

I CAN KNOW

The only right way to win a game is to follow the rules. God has rules in His Word, the Bible, that He wants you to obey.

I CAN LEARN

Put an X in the box to show who is following the rules.

NO RUNNING

I CAN PRAY

Tell God thank you for the rules He gives you. Ask Him to help you obey.

WEEK #50

I CAN KNOW

Even though Paul was in jail, the Word of God could not be chained. The good news about Jesus will always be told.

I CAN LEARN

You can tell others the Good News about Jesus, too. Write the name of someone on the envelope that you want to tell about Jesus.

I CAN PRAY

Pray for a missionary, like Paul, that you know.

WEEK #50

360

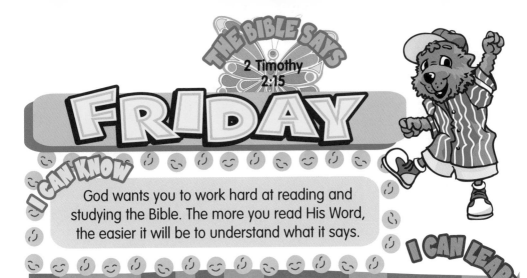

I CAN KNOW

God wants you to work hard at reading and studying the Bible. The more you read His Word, the easier it will be to understand what it says.

I CAN LEARN

Draw the hands on the clock to show when you read your Bible. Write the time on the line.

_____ : _____

I CAN PRAY

Ask God to help you understand the Bible.

WEEK #50

I CAN KNOW

God wants you to be kind to everyone.

I CAN LEARN

Draw a ⭕ around the 5 things in the bottom picture that are different.

WAY TO GO!

I CAN PRAY

Ask God to help you be kind to others today.

WEEK #50

362

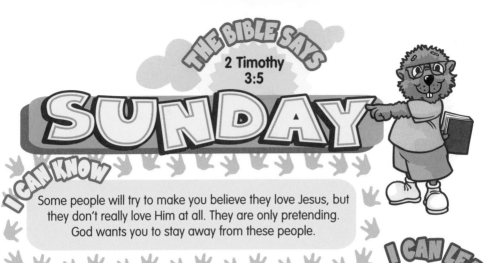

I CAN KNOW

Some people will try to make you believe they love Jesus, but they don't really love Him at all. They are only pretending. God wants you to stay away from these people.

I CAN LEARN

Draw a circle around the objects that are real. Put an X over the objects that are pretend.

I CAN PRAY

Ask God to help you choose the right friends.

WEEK #51

363

Doing the right thing is not always easy, but doing the right thing always makes God happy.

Draw a line to match the faces with the pictures.

WEEK #51

Ask God for the strength to do the right thing.

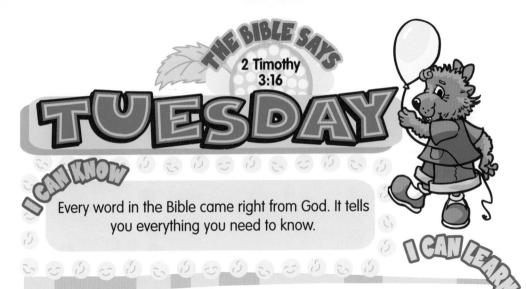

I CAN KNOW

Every word in the Bible came right from God. It tells you everything you need to know.

I CAN LEARN

Write the beginning letter sound of each picture on the line above it. Write your name on the last line.

The Bible is

___ ___ ___ ' ___ Word

to _____ .

I CAN PRAY

Tell God thank you for the Bible.

WEDNESDAY

I CAN KNOW

You should always be ready to share the Good News of Jesus with others. Never stop telling others about Him.

I CAN LEARN

You need to always be ready to tell others about Jesus. Draw a line from the word to the picture that matches the word.

Winter   Spring   Summer   Fall

I CAN PRAY

Ask God to help you tell a friend about Him today.

WEEK #51

God doesn't want you to ever stop telling people about Jesus. You can be a missionary wherever you are.

I CAN LEARN

Draw a line to help the children tell others in their town about Jesus.

I CAN PRAY

Pray for the people in your family that don't know about Jesus.

WEEK #51

367

FRIDAY

I CAN KNOW

Paul told Timothy to stay away from Alexander. He was not a good friend.

I CAN LEARN

God wants you to choose your friends wisely. He wants you to be a good friend to others. Friend begins with the letter sound F. Draw a △ around the pictures that begin with the same letter sound as friend. Write the letter F on the line.

I CAN PRAY

Ask God to help you be a good friend.

I CAN KNOW

Paul had to stand up for what was right all by himself, but God was with Him.

I CAN LEARN

You will never be alone. Use the code to write who will always be with you.

G =

O =

D =

WAY TO GO!

I CAN PRAY

Tell God thank you for always being with you.

SUNDAY

I CAN KNOW

You can count on God when you are in trouble. He cares for you.

I CAN LEARN

Draw a ⭕ around the picture that shows when you need to trust God.

I CAN PRAY

Tell God thank you for caring for you when you are in trouble.

WEEK #52

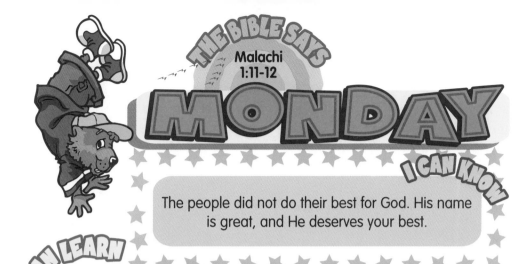

Malachi
1:11-12

MONDAY

I CAN KNOW

The people did not do their best for God. His name is great, and He deserves your best.

I CAN LEARN

You should do your quiet time in the morning before you start your day. Write a 1 by what happened first. Write a 2 by what happened next. Write a 3 by what happened last.

I CAN PRAY

Ask God to help you do your best for Him today.

WEEK #52

I CAN KNOW

Pastors are God's messengers. They should speak the truth.

I CAN LEARN

You can be God's messenger, too. Draw a circle around the places where you can be God's messenger.

I CAN PRAY

WEEK #52

Ask God to help your pastor always speak the truth.

WEDNESDAY

I CAN KNOW

You should not think that sin is good. It is wrong and hurts God.

I CAN LEARN

You need to obey God. This makes God happy. Draw a line from the face to the picture.

I CAN PRAY

Ask God to help you obey Him.

WEEK #52

373

I CAN KNOW

God never changes. He is always the same.

I CAN LEARN

Draw a ———— under the picture that is different in each row. Trace the word to see who is always the same.

I CAN PRAY

Tell God thank you that you can count on Him always being the same.

WEEK #52

374

FRIDAY

I CAN KNOW

God wants you to give Him what He deserves. When you give Him an offering, it will make you happy.

I CAN LEARN

Draw a circle around the things that you can give to God as an offering.

I CAN PRAY

WEEK #52

Ask God to help you be a cheerful giver.

375

Some people remained faithful to God. He did not forget this. He counted them His special treasures.

Draw a line to match the jewel to the treasure box it belongs in.

God loves you

God's child

Special

WAY TO GO!

Tell God thank you for making you special.

To Gopher Buddies Club Members

So that all club and family members will be on the same passages, the following dates correspond to the weekly passages. These dates are used for all Word of Life Quiet Times and daily radio broadcasts.

Week 1	Aug 28 - Sep 3	Psalms 120:1-126:6
Week 2	Sep 4 - Sep 10	Psalms 127:1-134:3
Week 3	Sep 11 - Sep 17	Psalms 135:1-139:12
Week 4	Sep 18 - Sep 24	Psalms 139:13-145:9
Week 5	Sep 25 - Oct 1	Psalms 145:10-150:6
Week 6	Oct 2 - Oct 8	1 Timothy 1:1-4:8
Week 7	Oct 9 - Oct 15	1 Timothy 4:9-6:21
Week 8	Oct 16 - Oct 22	Proverbs 26:1-28:28
Week 9	Oct 23 - Oct 29	Proverbs 29:1-31:31
Week 10	Oct 30 - Nov 5	Galatians 1:1-3:9
Week 11	Nov 6 - Nov 12	Galatians 3:10-5:1
Week 12	Nov 13 - Nov 19	Galatians 5:2-6:18
Week 13	Nov 20 - Nov 26	Daniel 1:1-2:49
Week 14	Nov 27 - Dec 3	Daniel 3:1-5:16
Week 15	Dec 4 - Dec 10	Daniel 5:17-8:27
Week 16	Dec 11 - Dec 17	Daniel 9:1-12:13
Week 17	Dec 18 - Dec 24	2 Peter 1:1-2:22
Week 18	Dec 25 - Dec 31	2 Peter 3:1-Jude 25
Week 19	Jan 1 - Jan 7	Jeremiah 1:1-5:31
Week 20	Jan 8 - Jan 14	Jeremiah 6:10-10:23
Week 21	Jan 15 - Jan 21	Jeremiah 12:1-20:18
Week 22	Jan 22 - Jan 28	Jeremiah 21:1-27:15
Week 23	Jan 29 - Feb 4	Jeremiah 28:1-32:27
Week 24	Feb 5 - Feb 11	Jeremiah 32:28-50:20
Week 25	Feb 12 - Feb 18	Acts 1:1-3:11
Week 26	Feb 19 - Feb 25	Acts 3:12-5:32
Week 27	Feb 26 - Mar 4	Acts 5:33-8:13
Week 28	Mar 5 - Mar 11	Acts 8:14-10:8
Week 29	Mar 12 - Mar 18	Acts 10:9-12:25
Week 30	Mar 19 - Mar 25	Acts 13:1-15:12
Week 31	Mar 26 - Apr 1	Acts 15:13-17:21
Week 32	Apr 2 - Apr 8	Acts 17:22-20:12
Week 33	Apr 9 - Apr 15	Acts 20:13-22:30
Week 34	Apr 16 - Apr 22	Acts 23:1-25:27
Week 35	Apr 23 - Apr 29	Acts 26:1-28:31
Week 36	Apr 30 - May 6	Habakkuk 1:1-Zephaniah 3:17
Week 37	May 7 - May 13	Deuteronomy 1:1-4:40
Week 38	May 14 - May 20	Deuteronomy 5:1-9:12
Week 39	May 21 - May 27	Deuteronomy 9:13-16:17
Week 40	May 28 - Jun 3	Deuteronomy 18:9-34:12
Week 41	Jun 4 - Jun 10	Job 1:1-10:22
Week 42	Jun 11 - Jun 17	Job 12:1-23:12
Week 43	Jun 18 - Jun 24	Job 26:1-42:17
Week 44	Jun 25 - Jul 1	1 John 1:1-2:27
Week 45	Jul 2 - Jul 8	1 John 2:28-4:21
Week 46	Jul 9 - Jul 15	1 John 5:1-3 John 14
Week 47	Jul 16 - Jul 22	1 Thessalonians 1:1-3:13
Week 48	Jul 23 - Jul 29	1 Thessalonians 4:1-5:28
Week 49	Jul 30 - Aug 5	2 Thessalonians 1:1-3:18
Week 50	Aug 6 - Aug 12	Colossians 1:1-2:15
Week 51	Aug 13 - Aug 19	Colossians 2:16-4:18
Week 52	Aug 20 - Aug 26	Joel 1:1-3:21

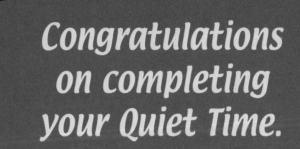

Congratulations on completing your Quiet Time.

Your Name

Parent's Name

Teacher's Name